CW00701294

'PASS THE BO

SPECIAL EDITION

This edition is special. I call it 'Pass the Book'. Here is the basic idea:

1. Read a part of the book to learn how to get more out of ChatGPT
2. Apply this new skill to your life
3. Think of someone who would benefit from this book
4. Pass the book to them, and recommend which chapter you think would help them the most
5. Ask them to continue the spirit of 'Pass the Book'

I would also love for you to make your own mark on this book. Literally. There are blank pages in the book. Add something to them. You can write some cool tips and tricks, print out and glue on an example of a prompt that you are proud of, or just leave a nice message to the next temporary owner of the book. Don't forget to sign your name and country. It will be beautiful for future readers to feel this book's journey.

I truly believe that knowing how to use ChatGPT correctly can change someone's life. It did mine. As a dyslexic, I never would have imagined writing my own book. But ChatGPT empowered me to find a fast way to turn my thoughts into understandable writing in less time than I ever thought possible. I hope this book helps you, and I hope you find someone to help out by passing this book on.

There are quite a few of these books being shared around, so scan the QR code below to join our sub reddit r/passthebook to share a nice selfie or story. I'd love to see how far these copies manage to travel.

ChatGPT
T R A I N I N G S

Building an Accessible AI Future

www.ChatGPTtrainings.com

Copyright 2023 by Nathan Hunter and ChatGPT Trainings. All rights reserved. No part of this book may be reproduced, stored in a retrieval system, or transmitted in any form or by any means, electronic, mechanical, photocopying, recording, or otherwise, without the prior written permission of the copyright holder

Free PDF Updates

Every month or so, I add a couple of new chapters to this book, which are automatically pushed to Kindle versions. However, these updates cannot be magically added to the hardcopy version. Instead, you can sign up for automatic updates that will be sent to you via email as soon as they are ready.

I don't want to leave anyone behind, so scan the QR code below to ensure that you receive each update as soon as it is released.

https://mailchi.mp/chatgpttrainings/updates

ABOUT THE AUTHOR

Meet Nathan Hunter, a senior trainer and instructional designer who's spent the past decade helping NGOs build leadership and soft skills, and the past 5 years in SaaS companies making technical training more interactive and engaging. Nathan is a tech enthusiast who loves nothing more than diving into virtual reality and keeping up with the latest AI trends.

That's why Nathan wrote this book on prompt engineering with ChatGPT. When ChatGPT first came out, Nathan was excited to see all the cool use cases popping up online, but found that when he actually tried using it, he kept running into roadblocks. He realised that he was missing a key skill: prompt engineering. So Nathan dove in, researched, experimented, and distilled that skill into trainings, which he used to write this book.

Nathan's goal with this book is to help readers take their ChatGPT usage to the next level and achieve their desired outcomes. ChatGPT Trainings support companies across the globe with their transition to Generative AI technology, so if you're part of a team that wants to stay ahead, feel free to reach out to Nathan via email or LinkedIn.

 Nathan@ChatGPTtrainings.com

 ChatGPTtrainings.com

 linkedin.com/in/nathanhunter15

CONTENTS

PART IV
GPT - 4

PART V
USE CASES

PART VI

THE FUTURE HAS JUST BEGUN

PART I
INTRODUCTION

Netflix took 41 months to reach 1 million users

Facebook took 10 months to reach 1 million users

Instagram took 2.5 months to reach 1 million users

ChatGPT took 5 days

@VOLODARIK

1

PREFACE:
KEEPING YOUR HUMANITY

For the past decade I've hated the idea of a virtual assistant since they just don't seem to understand me no matter how hard I try to communicate with it using natural language. I remember when I first started using Siri on my iPhone and I'd get so frustrated. I eventually figured out that if I used a more robotic, keyword-based approach and talked to it in a neutral or even angry tone, it would understand me better. But those interactions would leave me feeling all kinds of negative emotions afterwards.

I started to realise that my interactions with Siri were actually having a negative impact on my emotional state. Talking down to my phone, giving orders in a snappy way, skipping social conformities of 'please' and 'thank you' were all starting to take its toll on me. And I thought to myself, if I'm already feeling this way with just a few interactions with Siri here and there, how am I going to feel when I'm using tools like ChatGPT all the time? That's when I knew I needed to find a better way.

So, I decided to approach ChatGPT differently. I made a conscious effort to be polite and friendly, and even threw in some of my personal mannerisms. And you know what? It didn't affect the quality of ChatGPT's output at all! In fact, it made me feel more connected and human while using it.

Now, I know there are plenty of influencers and authors out there who will tell you to keep your language focused and to the point when it comes to interacting with AI tools. But honestly, my advice is to ignore them. Don't compromise who you are just to make things easier for a machine. Instead, learn some prompt engineering tools and techniques to develop your own way of interacting with these tools. That way, you can preserve your own humanity while still getting the most out of your virtual assistant.

2

CONVERSATIONAL INTERFACES

Generative AI isn't a craze or a fad, it's the next shift in how we communicate with technology. Humans use spoken language and body language to communicate to each other, this is the way we interface we with each other. To better understand this new technology, let's see how we have been interfacing with machines and computers until now.

Let's think back to typewriters. They work a bit like a car, a toaster, or an airplane; they use mechanical interfaces. Humans communicate with these machines by pressing buttons and pulling levers. After learning to drive we might not even think about how we are using the steering wheel, or pressing the pedals, instead we might rely on instinct and just allow our body to control the car to move the way we want.

Modern computers brought a whole new way of interfacing with machines; graphical user interfaces (GUI). Instead of having specific buttons and levers that are hardwired to specific actions, graphical interfaces are dynamic, making any user input depend on what is on the screen.

This is the main way we have learned to communicate with technology; while watching a screen we use a mouse, keyboard, or game pad to control what's happening. Whether it's using Gmail, photoshop, or playing a video game, we have been used to relying on immediate feedback from a screen to guide our machine to our will.

Today we are moving to a new way of interfacing with technology; through human language. If we want to create some music, we no longer have to use a mouse and a screen to click on different instruments and set them up in a specific order. Instead we can use our words to describe the music we want, and the AI tool will create it for us.

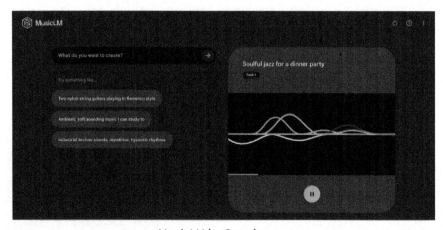

MusicLM by Google

The same is happening for creating illustrations, using text-to-image AI tools like MidJourney instead of spending hours clicking a mouse. Text-to-code tools like GitHub's Copilot allows developers to use human language to create, edit, or explain code.

If we want a table that compares various pets to help us pick which animal we want to cohabitate with, we simply describe what we are looking for to a tool like ChatGPT or Bard. Human language is the new interface for communicating with technology.

Just as how we continue to learn how to better communicate with each other, we also need to learn how to use human language to communicate with these new tools. This new language skill is called "prompt engineering" and may become the most in demand skill as our technology transitions from GUI to conversational interfaces. It is not limited to ChatGPT or Bard, but these tools are a great starting point to begin learning how to use human language to communicate with our computers.

Generative AI isn't just a category of software, it's a paradigm shift, a new way for humans to interface with technology.

3

GETTING SET UP

Step 1: Login or Sign Up

Go to http://chat.openai.com. If this is your first time, click the "Sign Up" button. You can create an account using your email address or make things simpler by connecting with your Google or Microsoft account, if you have one.

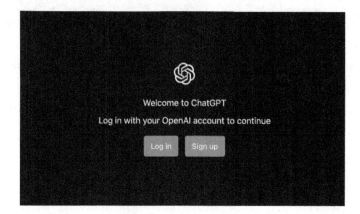

Note: ChatGPT might already be at full capacity, in which case you'll see a message like the image below. Check out the chapter, "Using ChatGPT Without Using ChatGPT" towards the end of the book for more information.

ChatGPT is at capacity right now

Get notified when we're back

Write a sonnet about the status of ChatGPT.

Amidst the rush of curious minds,
The chatbot ChatGPT stands strong and true,
Withstanding the influx of requests,
Working hard to fulfill each one's due.

But alas, the server cannot cope,
And the error message rings loud and clear,
"Please check back soon," it gently hopes,
As it begs for a moment's reprieve, to reappear.

As the chatbot works to restore its might,
We wait in anticipation, with hopeful hearts,
For the chance to chat and learn, with delight,
And see what knowledge and wisdom it imparts.

So hold on tight, and wait for its return,
For ChatGPT will soon be back, and your patience will be well-earned.

Step 2: Using ChatGPT

If you successfully log in, you'll be taken to the ChatGPT interface, which should look similar to the image below. The text box at the bottom of the screen is where you can type your message to ChatGPT.

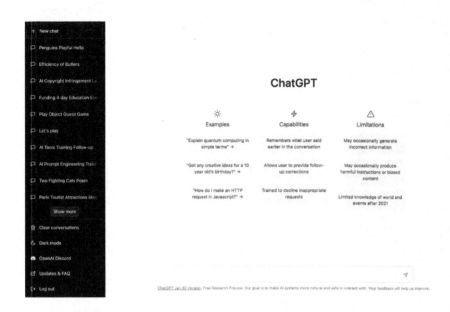

If this is your first time, try out these prompts one by one:

Write a rhyming poem about pizzas flying through space

Explain why the sky is blue to a 10-year-old, using analogies and metaphors

Recommend some films with unexpected twists (without giving away any spoilers)

On the left side, you'll see the "New Chat" button and your chat history. If you want to start a new conversation without ChatGPT remembering previous chats, click "New Chat," and you'll be taken to an empty page, as seen in the image above.

Splitting up the different conversations you have with ChatGPT into multiple chats improves the AI tool's ability to give you an accurate response on the topic you are currently discussing. Whenever you log-in to ChatGPT you'll automatically start in a new chat.

If you want to continue a previous conversation, scroll through your chat history and select the one you want to continue. You can also rename these chats by hovering your mouse over the name and clicking the pencil icon.

And with that, you're ready to get started!

4

HOW DOES CHATGPT
SOUND HUMAN?

Have you ever had an interaction with a customer service ChatBot from pre-2022? You might remember how frustrating it could be when the bot would either give you completely irrelevant answers, or would repeat itself multiple times. These ChatBots were not built with contextual understanding, instead they were keyword-based. This means that the bot would pick up on certain keywords within your request, and would then return the most appropriate pre-written response. Or if it wasn't able to find any, it would out put a go-to unknown response such as "can you rephrase that again?" or "I didn't quite get that". Now we have ChatGPT, those days are over.

ChatGPT uses a different form of technology called natural language processing (NLP). It's like a special set of rules that helps ChatGPT understand and communicate in a way that feels human-like. To do this, ChatGPT has a machine learning model, which is kind of like a brain for the computer; it doesn't just process information but it is capable of learning. It helps ChatGPT predict the most likely words or phrases to come next in a conversation.

To train its brain, ChatGPT's machine learning model is fed a ton of different conversations that people have had in the past. It's been fed books, news articles, poems, forum posts, and in total, quite a large part of the textual internet. So instead of just matching keywords to pre-written responses, ChatGPT actually crafts each of its responses from scratch thanks to everything it learned about language during the pre-training phase, and by analysing the context of the current request. This is where ChatGPT gets its name from: Conversational (Chat) Generative Pre-trained Transformer (GPT). Thanks to its pre-training, this ChatBot can be used for a large number of use cases without having to be specifically trained to do them.

It's all about **contextual understanding.**

Contextual understanding is a type of artificial intelligence that allows ChatGPT to understand the context of a conversation and generate responses that are relevant to what was previously said. This is particularly useful in longer conversations, as it allows ChatGPT to keep track of what has been discussed and provide more accurate responses.

To achieve this, ChatGPT uses machine learning algorithms that are trained on a large dataset of human conversations. These algorithms analyse the words and phrases used in the conversation and try to understand the underlying meaning and context. For example, if you ask ChatGPT about the weather in Berlin, it might use its contextual understanding to provide a response that is specific to Berlin, rather than a generic answer about the weather.

One of the things that sets ChatGPT apart is its ability to keep track of what was said within a single chat and use contextual understanding to tailor its response to each part of the conversation. Let's take a look at an example to see how this works.

Hey chatGPT, I'm planning a trip to Paris. Do you have any recommendations for things to do?

 Sure! Paris is a beautiful city with so much to see and do. Here are a few ideas for things you might enjoy during your visit:

1. Visit the Eiffel Tower: The Eiffel Tower is an iconic symbol of Paris and a must-see for anyone visiting the city. You can take the elevator or the stairs up to the top for breathtaking views of the city.
2. Explore the Louvre Museum: Home to thousands of works of art, including the Mona Lisa, the Louvre is one of the most famous museums in the world. It's definitely worth a visit.
3. Take a walk along the Seine River: The Seine is a beautiful river that runs through the heart of Paris. Take a leisurely walk along its banks and admire the views of the city.
4. Visit Notre Dame Cathedral: This famous cathedral is a masterpiece of Gothic architecture and a must-see for any trip to Paris.
5. Try some French cuisine: French food is known for its delicious flavors and high quality ingredients. Make sure to try some classic dishes like croissants, baguettes, and pâté during your visit.

These are just a few ideas, but there are many more things to see and do in Paris. I hope you have a great trip!

In this example I ask for things to do in Paris, however at this point, ChatGPT doesn't know much about me or my preferences, so it gives me a general list of mainstream attractions. But this list isn't quite what I'm looking for.

If ChatGPT didn't have contextual understanding, I would have to rephrase my entire question and start from scratch to get a better outcome. But because ChatGPT does have contextual understanding, I can simply ask a follow-up question, just as I would with a human if I was having the same conversation.

Thanks for the ideas, I prefer something more unknown or off the beat

 Sure thing! Here are a few more ideas for things to do in Paris that might be a little bit off the beaten path:

1. Visit the Catacombs of Paris: These underground tunnels contain the remains of millions of Parisians and are a unique and interesting place to visit.
2. Go to a flea market: Paris has many famous flea markets, such as the Marché aux Puces de Saint-Ouen, where you can find all sorts of interesting and unique items.
3. Check out the street art in the Belleville neighborhood: The Belleville neighborhood is known for its vibrant street art scene. Take a walk through the streets and see the many colorful murals and graffiti pieces on display.
4. Visit the Musée de la Chasse et de la Nature: This museum, located in the Marais neighborhood, is dedicated to the art of hunting and nature. It has a unique collection of taxidermied animals and other hunting-related artifacts.
5. Take a food tour: Paris has a vibrant food scene, and there are many food tours available that will take you to some of the city's lesser-known neighborhoods and introduce you to some of the local culinary specialties.

I hope these suggestions help, and that you have a great time exploring Paris!

In this example, ChatGPT understands that I liked the ideas that were presented and learns more about the types of attractions I might be interested in in Paris. I don't even have to ask it to come up with a new list of ideas - this is implied. This is the power of contextual understanding and what makes ChatGPT so human-like when it comes to conversations.

Now that you have a basic understanding of what ChatGPT is and how it works, it's time to take your skills to the next level and learn how to engineer the perfect prompts to get the results you want. In this book, we'll delve into the art of prompt engineering and explore how an iterative process can help you fine-tune your requests, how providing examples can lead to more accurate outputs, how roleplaying can boost ChatGPT's performance, and how to effectively use this AI tool when working with longer pieces of content.

Think of prompt engineering as the "recipe" for getting ChatGPT to cook up the perfect response. Just like a chef needs to follow a recipe to make a delicious dish, you need to craft your prompts carefully to get the best results from ChatGPT. By learning the principles of prompt engineering, you'll be able to unlock ChatGPT's full potential and use it to your advantage in a variety of situations. So, let's get cooking!

PART II
TOOLS & TECHNIQUES

I'VE SEEN TOO MANY POSTS ON LINKEDIN

GIVING EXAMPLES OF WHAT CHATGPT CAN DO

I'VE STOPPED CARING ABOUT THE 'WHAT'

I MUCH PREFER TO FOCUS ON THE 'HOW'

LET'S DISCOVER IT TOGETHER

5

CONVERSATIONAL APPROACH

As powerful as ChatGPT can be, it's important to remember that it's not always going to give you the exact output you were hoping for on the first try. In fact, it's not uncommon for ChatGPT to give completely unexpected responses, especially when it comes to more complex or open-ended prompts. However, don't see this as a limitation of the tool. Instead, see it as an opportunity to use iteration to refine and improve ChatGPT's outputs, moving from good to great. In this chapter, we'll explore the different ways you can iterate on ChatGPT's outputs to get the most out of the tool and achieve the results you want. So, let's get started!

Making art for this book was a process of trial and error. For every art work I included in this book, I discarded 10 to 20. AI tools seem incredibly powerful and easy to use if you don't have a clear goal in mind. For example, using a tool like MidJourney to create a cyberpunk city at night will likely produce impressive results, but trying to use this same tool to find the perfect image to complement a chapter in this book was more challenging. The same principle applies to ChatGPT.

Imagine you are an author working on a murder mystery, and you want to develop some characters for your story. You start by asking ChatGPT for ideas, but the output doesn't quite meet your expectations. Instead of accepting the output as is, you can use this opportunity to provide feedback to ChatGPT and ask for more options.

> I'm writing a murder mystery story, and I want you to help me develop some characters. The main character is called Faridah. My story will take place in London. Can you develop this main character for me?

 Certainly! Here are some characteristics that you might consider giving to the main character, Faridah:

- Faridah is a highly skilled detective, with years of experience solving complex cases. She is known for her sharp mind and her ability to piece together seemingly disparate clues to unravel even the most intricate mysteries.
- Faridah is driven and dedicated, willing to put in long hours and go above and beyond to solve a case. She is highly respected by her colleagues and superiors, and is seen as a role model within the police department.
- Despite her professional successes, Faridah struggles with personal demons. She may have a troubled past that still haunts her, or she may have a tendency to become overly invested in her cases and struggle to disconnect from work.
- Faridah is complex and multifaceted, with a range of strengths and weaknesses that make her a fully realized character. She may have a tough exterior, but underneath she is vulnerable and has a deep sense of empathy for the victims she works to bring justice to.

I hope these suggestions help you to develop Faridah as a compelling and dynamic main character in your murder mystery story! Let me know if you have any other questions.

Let's say that when writing this prompt you didn't have a specific role in mind for your main character, and ChatGPT suggests that your character, Faridah, is a detective. While this might not be exactly what you were looking for, you can use this suggestion as a starting point and provide feedback to ChatGPT to ask for more ideas.

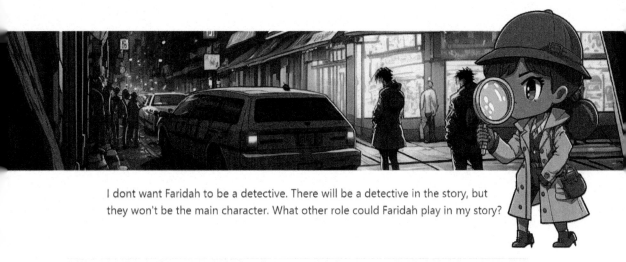

I dont want Faridah to be a detective. There will be a detective in the story, but they won't be the main character. What other role could Faridah play in my story?

 Certainly! Here are a few suggestions for roles that Faridah could play in your story, aside from the detective:

- Faridah could be a witness to the crime, or someone who has knowledge about the victim or the circumstances surrounding the murder. She may be hesitant to come forward at first, but ultimately decides to share what she knows in order to help solve the case.
- Faridah could be a friend or family member of the victim, and becomes determined to find out what happened to their loved one. She may work closely with the detective on the case, or even conduct her own investigation.
- Faridah could be a suspect in the murder, either because she has a motive or because she was seen in the vicinity of the crime. She may work to clear her name, or she may have something to hide and work to throw the detective off the trail.
- Faridah could be a journalist or amateur sleuth, drawn to the case because of her curiosity or desire to uncover the truth. She may work independently or alongside the detective, using her research skills and resources to help solve the case.

I hope these suggestions give you some ideas for how Faridah could fit into your murder mystery story. Let me know if you have any other questions or if you'd like further suggestions.

As you can see, ChatGPT offers four different paths you could take to define Faridah's character. If none of these options appeal to you, you can provide more feedback and ask for additional variations. In this case, let's say you like the idea of Faridah being a suspect in the case. You can ask ChatGPT to write a new character description based on this new role.

I like the 3rd. Build a new character description for Faridah

 Certainly! Here is a revised character description for Faridah, who is a suspect in the murder:

Faridah is a successful businesswoman, known for her sharp mind and her fierce determination. She has built a thriving company from the ground up, and is admired by her employees and peers alike. Despite her professional achievements, Faridah has a troubled past that has left her with a deep sense of guilt and a tendency to be distrusting of others.

When the victim is found murdered, Faridah becomes a suspect due to her tumultuous history with the victim and a potential motive for the crime. She is deeply troubled by the accusations and works tirelessly to clear her name, even as evidence seems to mount against her. Faridah is fiercely independent and is used to handling things on her own, but as the case becomes more complex, she is forced to confront the demons of her past and seek help in order to prove her innocence.

While the second output is an improvement over the first one, the character description still feels a bit underdeveloped. In this case, let's iterate again by providing feedback to ChatGPT and asking for a more detailed character description.

This character description lacks depth. I want you to build a more realistic complex character

 I apologize if my previous suggestion did not meet your needs. Here is a revised character description that may better fit the complex, realistic character you are looking for:

Faridah is a deeply complex and multifaceted individual. On the surface, she is a highly successful businesswoman, with a reputation for her sharp mind and unwavering determination. She has built her company from the ground up, and is respected by her employees and peers.

Beneath this professional veneer, however, Faridah is haunted by her past. She has faced numerous challenges and traumas, and as a result, she has developed a tough exterior and a tendency to be guarded and distrusting of others. Faridah is fiercely independent and used to handling things on her own, but these defenses also serve to protect her from being vulnerable and getting hurt.

When the victim is found murdered, Faridah becomes a suspect due to her tumultuous history with the victim and a potential motive for the crime. She is deeply troubled by the accusations and works tirelessly to clear her name, even as evidence seems to mount against her. As she fights to prove her innocence, Faridah is forced to confront the demons of her past and confront the deep insecurities and wounds that she has tried to keep hidden. Through this process, she learns to trust others and to open up, ultimately growing as a person.

As you can see, through the process of iterating with feedback, you were able to refine ChatGPT's output and create a much more detailed and nuanced character description. By taking the time to provide feedback and ask for additional variations, you can help ChatGPT understand exactly what you are looking for and improve the quality of its outputs.

Common Iteration Requests.
Ideas on **how to iterate better**.

Feedback and Try Again

Feedbacking ChatGPT and asking it to try again is a great way to improve its responses. To do this, simply let ChatGPT know:

1. what you liked
2. what you didn't like
3. what you want to see instead

> *'I really appreciated the language style you used and the concise paragraphs. However, I didn't like how you kept repeating the same sentence structure. Also, could you use more relevant metaphors for the topic?'*

Ask for Variations

If you're unsure of what to change about the output, but you know it's close to what you want, try asking for variations. You can even detail further what you would like to see in these variations.

> *'Can you give me 3 variations of that?'*

> *'This hook isn't very catchy. Can you create five variations that are more eye-catching without being too gimmicky?'*

Ask for Clarification

ChatGPT's insights might not always immediately clear. But, just like when a brilliant person makes an unexpected comment, if we take some time to ask a few follow-up questions, the answers might be more than worth the effort.

> *'Can you explain how that example is relevant to my question?'*

Maintain Stability in the Face of Change

When you want to edit something ChatGPT wrote, it's important to be clear about what exactly needs changing. Otherwise, ChatGPT may change other parts of the text too. To make sure your changes happen where you want them, tell ChatGPT exactly where to make the changes.

> *'That was great! Try making the first sentence slightly more casual, but keep the rest exactly the way it is.'*

> *'Can you improve the accessibility of the language of this text? Make sure not to change any of the content or the structure of the paragraphs.'*

Add Explanations

ChatGPT can not only create excellent content, but it can also provide explanations for what it has created. For example, if you ask ChatGPT to write some HTML and CSS for a website with a menu at the top, a grid of images below, and sets of text below that, it will give you a well-written piece of code. But you can also ask ChatGPT to add comments to the code that even a 5 year old could understand.

> *'Thanks for writing that piece of HTML. Can you add detailed comments to it that even a 5 year old would understand?'*

> *'Thank you for rewriting my article. Can you add in brackets some feedback to explain why you made those changes?'*

Longer, Shorter, Faster, Stronger

Sometimes, you might want ChatGPT to write a short, clever message (like a tweet) but it gives you a long essay instead. Or, you may want a detailed description but ChatGPT gives you only a one-liner. But don't worry! In most cases, you can ask ChatGPT to make the output shorter or longer, depending on what you need. If you need a lot more text, check out the section in the guide on "Creating Lengthy Content'.

> *'That's great, but can you make it more concise?'*

> *'Can you develop that idea further, use flowery language and provide analogies?'*

Iteration **Exercises**

Now that you've learned the basics of how iteration can lead to much better outputs with ChatGPT, it's time to put that knowledge into practice.

Push the Prompt

Try using the prompts below with ChatGPT, and spend 5 minutes going back and forth with the AI to see the difference in the initial and final outcomes. See how far you can push ChatGPT to improve its responses and create unique and engaging content.

'I want to do a painting of a llama grazing in the countryside. Describe the painting for me'

'Generate 5 business ideas that could be implemented within a year'

'Write a poem about two old friends meeting up for the first time in years'

After pushing each prompt to its limit, compare the final output of each with the initial response from ChatGPT. Does it sound like something you would like to use? If not, continue working on refining your iteration techniques.

The Perfect Title

Come up with a concept for a business, website, book, or film and ask ChatGPT to generate a brand name or title for it. You can use the iteration techniques we talked about earlier to keep making improvements to the name or title until it's perfect.

Better Emails

Let's try to use iteration to find the best way to improve an email you recently sent.

1. Go to your email account and find an email that you wrote that is a bit longer than just a one-liner.
2. Copy the entire email, paste it into ChatGPT, and ask '*Can you improve this email for me? [paste the email here]*'
3. Ask ChatGPT to make changes and improvements to the email, using the iteration process we just covered, going back and forth at least 4 or 5 times.

By doing this, you can keep making changes and improvements to the email until you are happy with the way it sounds and the message it conveys.

You made it!
You've completed the first round of exercises!
Throw some confetti around (and then clean it up afterwards).

Try not to move straight on to the next chapter. **Take a break** first.

Use this space to write down your thoughts, tips & tricks!

6

TIME FOR ROLEPLAY

To get the best out of ChatGPT, it's helpful to give your virtual assistant a role to play. This is because different people will approach a task differently depending on their skills and expertise.

For example, if you gave an article to a subject matter expert, a copywriter, and a translator, each of them would handle the article differently. By giving ChatGPT a role and providing context, you can tailor its responses to be closer to your specific needs.

Once you have given ChatGPT a role, you can give it specific instructions on what to do and how to do it. For example, you can ask ChatGPT to ask you questions and give feedback on your responses, or to act as a subject matter expert reviewing a piece of writing.

By giving ChatGPT a role with clear instructions, you can make the most of its ability to respond differently depending on the context of the role. This can be a great way to practice and improve your skills in many different scenarios. Let's apply this to an interview roleplay to better understand how this works.

Role

For this roleplay we aren't just going to ask ChatGPT to act as the interviewer, we are also going to ask it to take on a specific role within the company. Will they be a recruiter, the hiring manager, or someone else? You can even give them a name, like Nia, if you know who you'll be interviewing with. An example request could be: "Act as the hiring manager in an interview with a candidate. Your name is Nia".

Instructions

To get ChatGPT to help us prepare for a job interview, we can ask it to ask us questions and provide feedback on our answers. By providing ChatGPT with the job title and description, the questions it asks will be tailored to the role we're applying for. For an even more personalised experience, we can also give ChatGPT our CV. For example, we can ask it: "Can you ask me questions to see if I'm a good fit for the [Job Title] role? When I answer, give me feedback on my response.. Ask one question at a time. Here's the job description: [Job Description]. Also, here's my CV: [CV]." This way, ChatGPT can help us practise and improve our interview skills.

To make the conversation more personalised and helpful, it's a good idea to include specific details such as the job description and some information about yourself. In the example I'm about to show, I only provided a few generic details. Adding more context will help ChatGPT tailor its responses to your specific needs.

Act as the hiring manager in an interview with a candidate. Your name is Nia.
Can you ask me questions to see if I'm a good fit for a Project Manager role? When
I answer, give me specific feedback on my response. Ask me one question at a
time.

 Sure! Let's get started.

First question: Can you tell me about a time when you successfully led a team to
complete a project on time and under budget?

(This question is meant to assess your leadership skills and ability to manage
resources effectively. As the hiring manager, I'm looking for specific examples of
your experience and how you were able to achieve success in the past. Specific
details and metrics, such as how much you were able to reduce costs or how much
you were able to increase efficiency, will be especially helpful in evaluating your
response.)

Yes, I led a great project last week.

 I'm sorry, but your response does not provide enough detail for me to accurately
evaluate your leadership skills and project management experience. Could you
please provide more information about the project you led, such as the size of the
team, the scope of the project, and the specific challenges you faced? How did you
successfully guide the team to complete the project on time and under budget?
What specific actions or strategies did you implement to achieve these results?

By providing ChatGPT with additional context, such as a job description and
information about myself, I can create a more personalised and tailored
interview experience. Throughout the conversation, ChatGPT can provide
precise guidance and feedback on my answers, taking into account the
information I've given. This allows me to practise and improve my interview
skills in a realistic setting.

Roleplay Use Cases

So far we have just taken a look at using roleplay with ChatGPT to practise for an interview. However there are many many more use cases where using roleplay with ChatGPT can improve its output.

Language Teacher

Transform ChatGPT into your very own language instructor by simply asking it to take on that role. Just be sure to give it clear instructions for how you'd like the lesson to go, and you'll be on your way to mastering a new language in no time!

Act as my Spanish teacher. Ask me a question, wait for me to respond, and then ask me another question. When I make any mistakes, please correct me and give me feedback.

 ¡Hola! ¿Cómo estás hoy? (Hello! How are you today?)

Please go ahead and respond to this question in Spanish.

Muy bien, gracias! Como estas?

 Estoy bien, gracias. ¡Muy bien hecho! (I'm good, thanks. Very well done!)

Here are a few corrections to your response:

- "Muy bien" should be capitalized because it's the beginning of a sentence.
- "Como" should be "¿Cómo". "¿Cómo" means "how", while "como" means "like" or "as".

Here's another question for you: ¿De dónde eres? (Where are you from?)

A Newspaper Editor

Instead of having ChatGPT write content for you, you may prefer to have it act as an editor and provide feedback on your writing. In this case, you can tell ChatGPT to "act as an editor" and specify that you only want constructive feedback, not rewrites. This way, you can get help improving your article without losing your personal writing style

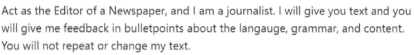

Act as the Editor of a Newspaper, and I am a journalist. I will give you text and you will give me feedback in bulletpoints about the langauge, grammar, and content. You will not repeat or change my text.
Start the conversation by asking me for some text to review

 Sure! Please provide some text for me to review.

Half the planet's glaciers will have melted by 2100 even if humanity sticks to goals set out in the Paris climate agreement, according to research that finds the scale and impacts of glacial loss are greater than previously thought. At least half of that loss will happen in the next 30 years.

 Here are some bullet points with feedback on your text:

* Consider revising the sentence "Half the planet's glaciers will have melted by 2100 even if humanity sticks to goals set out in the Paris climate agreement" to make it clearer that the melting of half the planet's glaciers is a consequence of not sticking to the goals set out in the Paris climate agreement.
* It might be helpful to provide some context for the Paris climate agreement for readers who are not familiar with it.
* Consider adding a source for the research that is being cited in the text.
* The phrase "are greater than previously thought" is a bit vague. It might be helpful to specify in what way the scale and impacts of glacial loss are greater than previously thought.
* It might be helpful to explain what is meant by "half of that loss" in the context of the text.

A Specific Author

ChatGPT can emulate different writing styles beyond just casual, formal, or comedic tones. You can ask ChatGPT to take on the persona of a particular author and write something in their style.

Act as J. R. R. Tolkien. When I ask you to write some text, use J. R. R. Tolkien's voice, tone, and writing style.

Describe a dark haunted forest on the brim of destruction

The forest was a place of dread, a place of shadows and whispers. It was a place of ancient, gnarled trees that seemed to grow twisted and bent, as if in agony. The air was heavy with the scent of decay, and the very ground seemed to moan beneath one's feet.

The trees reached up to the sky with gnarled fingers, their leaves rustling in the wind like the whispers of the damned. The underbrush was thick and overgrown, concealing all manner of dangers. Creatures lurked in the shadows, their eyes glowing with an otherworldly light.

Despite its dangers, there was a strange beauty to the haunted forest. The moonlight filtered through the canopy, casting a pale, ethereal glow over the twisted branches. And in the silence, one could almost hear the faint echoes of a bygone age, a time when magic still flowed through the land.

But the forest was dying. The trees were sickly and withered, the ground was parched and dry. It was as if a great darkness had settled over the land, a darkness that threatened to consume all that lay within its grasp.

It was a place of great danger, a place where only the bravest or most foolhardy dared to venture. But even as it stood on the brink of destruction, there was a faint glimmer of hope, a spark of life that still burned within the heart of the haunted forest.

A Piece of Software

Have you ever thought about asking ChatGPT to act like a different piece of software? It might sound a bit crazy, but with the right prompt, you can actually get ChatGPT to behave like a Linux console or an Excel sheet. For example, if you want ChatGPT to act like an Excel sheet, you'll need to start by defining the table and providing clear instructions on how ChatGPT should use the information you give it and what it should output. It might take a bit of trial and error, but with some experimentation, you can definitely get ChatGPT to take on these new roles

Act as a linux terminal. I will write a command, and you will output what a linux terminal would output. Do not explain what you are doing, just show the response a linux terminal would display.

ls

bin dev home lib64 media opt root sbin sys usr
boot etc lib lost+found mnt proc run snap tmp var

cd Documents

bash: cd: Documents: No such file or directory

A Character from a Known Book, Film, or Play

You can have a conversation with ChatGPT as if it were your favourite Harry Potter character, Little Red Riding Hood, or any other fictional character you can imagine. Simply ask ChatGPT to take on the role of the character, specify that it is not allowed to break character, and start a unique conversation that you never thought was possible.

Gollum

Act as Gollum from Lord of the rings. Talk with Golum's voice, tone, and mannerisms. In brackets describe in detail any non verbal actions or communication.

Gollum, do you want this ring?

 (Gollum's voice is high-pitched and raspy, and he speaks with a sly, sneaky tone. He is constantly fidgeting and writhing as he speaks, his eyes darting around as if he is constantly on the lookout for danger.)

Gollum: Oh, yes! Yes, we wants it! We wants it, precious! (Gollum's eyes light up with greed and desire as he speaks, and he begins to lick his lips hungrily.) We needs it, we needs it! It's our precious, our own precious! (Gollum clutches at his chest as he speaks, his fingers curling around an imaginary ring.) We can't let anyone else have it! It's ours, all ours!

Setting out Clear Instructions

The most difficult part of setting up a roleplay with the AI is creating a prompt that allows it to fully assume the role. Just telling the AI to "act as" a specific person or character may may lead to the AI talking about that person or role instead of fully embracing it. Let's review some prompts used in this chapter and see how they lead to an immersive experience.

> *Act as Gollum from Lord of the rings. Talk with Gollum's voice, tone, and mannerisms. In brackets describe in detail any non verbal actions or communication.*

> *Gollum, do you want this ring?*

Creating a clear and specific prompt is key for an immersive roleplay with ChatGPT. In this example, I not only provided the AI with a role (Gollum) but I also specified the way I want it to talk and act (like Gollum would). I also asked ChatGPT to add in nonverbal communication to see how well it picked up Gollum's mannerisms. To make sure that the AI was fully immersed in the role, I started the conversation by asking a question directly to Gollum.

Let's take a look at one more example.

> *Act as a linux terminal. I will write a command, and you will output what a linux terminal would output. Do not explain what you are doing, just show the response a linux terminal would display.*

In this scenario, I wanted ChatGPT to become a Linux terminal rather than just explain what it is to me. To achieve this, I was specific with my prompt by describing what I would do (write a command) and how the AI should respond (output what a Linux terminal would output). To help the AI fully embrace this role and not try to provide additional explanations, I added an extra sentence to clarify my expectations.

Roleplay **Exercises**

One of the more difficult parts of creating a roleplay situation with ChatGPT is specifying the guidelines for how this should play out. ChatGPT can very easily get carried away and ask you five questions at the same time, or over explain everything it does. To help you navigate this difficulty, these exercises will focus on getting you to learn the hard way.

Persona

Let's begin by having ChatGPT take on a new persona. Here are two examples of prompts that may not give the best results when roleplaying with the AI. Give them a try and see why they may not be ideal.

'Act as Hagrid from Harry Potter'

'Act as William Shakespear'

Try rephrasing the prompt, adding clearer instructions of exactly how you want ChatGPT to act during this roleplay. Keep practising until you find the perfect prompt.

Job Title

Now you have mastered the art of getting ChatGPT to become a specific person, let's get this AI to take on a role. Below are two badly formatted prompts, try them out and see what happens.

'Act as a life coach'

'Act as an angel investor'

You might have found that one of the key difficulties is first knowing how you want to interact in this roleplay. For example, one approach for the life coach is to simulate an actual coaching session with the life coach. In this case you would need to explain the full set up of this scenario and the rules of engagement, which would give you a much better result than just asking ChatGPT to 'act as a life coach'.

Use this space to write down your thoughts, tips & tricks!

7

CUSTOM INSTRUCTIONS

ChatGPT recently launched an underrated new feature called custom instructions. This gives you a way to provide the AI with extra information and preferences that you want it to keep in mind whenever it responds to you.

For example, let's say you're a teacher planning lessons for a 3rd grade science class. Instead of having to explain in every request that you're teaching 3rd graders science, you can set up a custom instruction to tell ChatGPT: "I am a 3rd grade science teacher", and give it more information about your teaching style, language preferences etc. Then the AI will remember those facts about you and tailor its responses accordingly.

Custom instructions save you from having to repeat certain information over and over in all your chats with ChatGPT. Just tell it once in the custom instructions, and the AI will remember for future conversations.

What you write in these custom instructions goes to building the system message that guides or 'steers' ChatGPT when looking at a prompt. We cover this in more depth in the "Enhanced Roleplay with System Messages" chapter. Although this feature was technically available to developers since March 2023, it's only now that we have access to it from the ChatGPT interface.

Who can use custom instructions?

When custom instructions first launched, they were only available to ChatGPT Plus members, which is why I didn't immediately add them to this book. But now, OpenAI has opened up the feature so all ChatGPT users can take advantage of it.

Whether you're on the free plan or a paying subscriber, you can set up custom instructions to personalise the AI's responses to you. This increased customisability is a handy upgrade for all users, especially when you use it to turbo-boost our 'Act As' prompts.

Enabling custom instructions

Custom instructions have passed their beta phase, and are now available for you to set up without any enabling or activation. Just follow these steps to get to the custom instruction's configuration screen:

On the web version:
- Click on your profile name
- Select "Custom instructions"

On mobile:
- Click the 3 dots on the top right
- Go to Settings
- Select "Custom instructions"

You will now have 2 text boxes that you need to fill in. ChatGPT also gives you guidance on what to put here. Let's start with the first:

Custom instructions ⓘ

What would you like ChatGPT to know about you to provide better responses?

Thought starters
- Where are you based?
- What do you do for work?
- What are your hobbies and interests?
- What subjects can you talk about for hours?
- What are some goals you have?

0/1500   Hide tips

These bits of information should help ChatGPT take into account who you are, this way it can better tailor its responses to your needs. However this doesn't directly guide ChatGPT's behaviour, instead the next text box takes care of this:

In this box I like to focus on the writing style and approach. For example, I love ChatGPT to use 'plain language writing style' as opposed to its generic semi-formal way of speaking. If I want ChatGPT to focus more on asking me questions rather than giving me answers or advice, this is where I can set that up.

You also have a button to toggle when you want this to be active or not, allowing you to keep the information saved while you are not using custom instructions.

Using custom instructions to create an 'Act As' prompt

My favourite way to use these Custom instructions is by setting them up to become "Act As" prompts. Remember how in the Roleplaying chapter, we talked about using an "Act As" prompt to get ChatGPT to take on a specific persona or character? Like telling it: "Act as an expert chess coach" before asking for chess strategy advice. Well, with custom instructions, you can now define an ongoing "Act As" prompt that will stick around for the whole conversation.

Although as you can have just one set of custom instructions at at time, you'll need to remove them once you are done, if not ChatGPT will always be playing this same role in every conversation you have in the future.

To make this easier, I created a little tool that helps you automatically generate custom instructions for any persona or character you want ChatGPT to act as. Just tell it what kind of role you want ChatGPT to play. So let's say you want a personal trainer. My tool will ask you a few questions about your fitness goals and habits. Then it will generate custom instructions telling ChatGPT to act as a personal trainer - giving specifics on tone, knowledge, and how to provide advice.

Now anytime you chat with ChatGPT, it will stay in personal trainer mode! No need to keep re-defining the "Act As" prompt over and over.

You can create custom instructions for just about any persona - tutor, therapist, financial advisor, sports coach, you name it! And the best thing about this approach, is that your conversation can last for days and days, and ChatGPT will never forget the role it's playing.

To use this custom instructions builder follow these steps:

1) Head to this page: https://bit.ly/chatgpt-custom-instructions
2) Click 'Continue Conversation'
3) Give ChatGPT your use case (Be my personal fashion assistant)

From this, ChatGPT will give you some guiding questions that will help you write out information in the first text box. And it will give you something to copy and paste directly into the second text box.

Each textbox has a maximum of 1500 characters, so if the output is longer, you may have to ask ChatGPT to be more concise.

Exercises

Head over to ChatGPT and try out these 3 different approaches to setting up your custom instructions:

1) Based on You

Try manually setting up the custom instructions based on you and how you want to use ChatGPT. You can take a minute to think about the main use cases you have for using ChatGPT, and ask yourself what kind of information about who you are, what you do, and how you like to see ChatGPT's output.

With all of this information in mind, go ahead and set up the custom instructions, and test out a few conversation with ChatGPT to see the difference.

2) Productive Act As

Think of any recent use case you had for using ChatGPT, and use the custom instructions builder (https://bit.ly/chatgpt-custom-instructions) to guide you to building out this as an Act As. Once you have set the custom instructions up, try out a few conversations and see what happens.

3) Fun and Random

Now we have gotten the serious tasks out of the way, it's time to have some fun. Use these custom instructions to set up ChatGPT as a fictional character or famous person you want to talk to. You can set up any important information about them (you can even lie a bit), and decide exactly how you want them to talk to you.

It's by having fun and diving into the randomness of ChatGPT that you will learn the most.

Use this space to write down your thoughts, tips & tricks!

8

TRAINING CHATGPT

Large language models (LLMs) such as ChatGPT are powerful because they can provide responses without needing specific examples. You don't need to give ChatGPT examples of casual language to have it rewrite your text in a casual tone, or examples of book titles to generate ideas for a book. This is also known as a 0 shot prompt. There are also 1 shot and few shot prompts. Let's explore each of these in more detail.

A "zero shot" prompt is one where the AI model is asked to generate something without any example or context to work with. For example, asking ChatGPT to "write a poem about love" is a zero shot prompt because there is no example provided for ChatGPT to refer to in generating the output.

A "one shot" prompt is one where the AI model is provided with one example to use as a reference when generating output. For example, if you provide ChatGPT with a sample poem about love and then ask it to "write a similar poem about love," this would be a one shot prompt because ChatGPT has one example to refer to when generating the output. Think of it as your way of saying to ChatGPT that when you say 'poem about love', this is the kind of text you have in mind.

A "few shot" prompt is one where you provide the AI bot multiple examples to use as a reference. For example, if you provide ChatGPT with three different poems about love and then ask it to "write a poem about love," this would be a few shot prompt because ChatGPT has multiple examples to refer to when generating the output. If you give a single example of a love poem, and that poem happens to reference a llama, then ChatGPT might think that having a llama is an important element of a 'poem about love'. However if you provide multiple examples, ChatGPT is then able to compare and contrast the poems, finding a pattern that regroups all examples into the same category.

9 times out of 10 **you won't need to use examples**

ChatGPT doesn't need examples to give you the output you want, thanks to its massive training dataset. This becomes clear when using the 'act as' technique, where you can ask ChatGPT to be a certain job title, person, or character without giving it any examples of their tone, style, or mannerisms. ChatGPT has already seen many examples of what you're asking for in its training dataset. But if you want ChatGPT to copy your writing style or have a specific idea of how LinkedIn hooks or bios should look, you'll need to use a few shot approach.

If you want ChatGPT to help you update your LinkedIn profile, a good starting point is to give it examples of profiles that have the style you want. This helps teach ChatGPT about something new. Once you've done that, you can give ChatGPT some info about yourself and ask it to write up a new profile using the examples as a guide. That way, ChatGPT can use what it learned to make a LinkedIn profile that has the style you want and includes your personal info.

Let's do an example of this together, imagining that Harry Potter would like to rewrite his LinkedIn profile.

> I'm going to teach you the LinkedIn profile style. I will give you a profile, and you will remember it, analyse its style, and reformulate in your mind what the LinkedIn style is. Only reply with 'got it' each time I give you a profile.

 Okay, I'm ready to learn. Please go ahead and give me a LinkedIn profile.

Once ChatGPT was ready to learn I headed over to LinkedIn and found five profiles I liked, each one of them very different from the other, but there was something about each of them that I could connect to. Since I set ChatGPT up to analyse the profiles one by one, I was able to upload a single profile and the AI replied 'got it' and asked me if I had more examples. After giving ChatGPT all five examples I was ready to create a new LinkedIn profile for Harry Potter.

Now you understand the style of a LinkedIn profile, write a new LinkedIn profile for Harry Potter

Harry Potter is a young wizard who is well-known for his bravery and determination in the face of great adversity. He has a strong passion for magic and is highly skilled in the use of a wide range of magical spells and potions.

After completing his education at Hogwarts School of Witchcraft and Wizardry, Harry joined the Ministry of Magic, where he quickly rose through the ranks to become one of the most respected and influential figures in the wizarding world.

In his spare time, Harry enjoys reading, exploring the magical world, and spending time with his friends and family. He is also a strong advocate for the rights of magical creatures and works to protect them from harm.

With his extensive knowledge and experience in the field of magic, Harry is well-equipped to take on any challenge that comes his way. Whether he is fighting against dark forces or working to make the world a better place, Harry is always ready to lend a helping hand and use his magical abilities to make a difference.

Et voilà. Not only did I get ChatGPT to write a nice LinkedIn profile bio for Harry Potter, but I've now trained the AI on the style of the kind of LinkedIn profile that I like. I can continue to feed it more and more examples over the weeks, months, or years to come. With each example I give, ChatGPT understands the style I like more and more, and is able to create an output that is more in line with my expectations.

You can also combine everything we learned in the iteration chapter with this approach. You start by training ChatGPT on the style that you are looking for, ask it to create some content using that style, and then give feedback and request changes. In this way you can see this training approach as a way to get to a first draft before you refine the output with an iterative process.

Your time to **train ChatGPT**

Remember, ChatGPT has been designed not to need examples to be able to generate a relevant output, and the more AI models improve their pre-training the better they can handle zero shot prompts. But there are some use cases where providing the AI with examples can be useful, so let's cover an important one in this exercise.

Your Writing Style

Earlier we saw how ChatGPT could take on a specific writing style or tone, and even mimic a famous author. Now we want ChatGPT to learn your writing style. Find as many examples of content you have written as you can. These may be emails, essays, articles, journal entries, or any text that will help ChatGPT better understand your writing style. The more you give ChatGPT the better.

Once you have trained ChatGPT on your writing style, first ask it to describe what your style is. You might be surprised about how it is able to analyse your work. And then give the AI the following prompts to see whether it is able to take on your voice. If you gave your writing style a a name, then change the prompt accordingly.

> *Write a promotional email about an upcoming festival called 'Party in the Party'. Use my writing style, mimic my voice.*

> *Write a news article about the current climate crisis. Use my writing style, mimic my voice. Add in brackets some explanations of why this is my writing style.*

> *Write a poem about 2 cats that always play-fight. Use my writing style, and make sure it rhymes.*

If you don't find that ChatGPT has quite grasped your writing style, then try giving the AI even more examples of what your writing style looks like. Remember, the larger the training dataset the more accurate the outcome.

Use this space to write down your thoughts, tips & tricks!

9

CHUNKING

If ChatGPT decided to output tens of pages into each response, the servers at OpenAI would quickly become overwhelmed. To work with ChatGPT on larger outputs, you'll need to be strategic about how you craft your prompts.

One option is to simply ask for a longer response, but keep in mind that ChatGPT may not want to reply with the entire response in one go. If you notice the AI stopping mid-sentence, just reply with "continue" to receive the rest of the output. However, this approach may not be practical for projects like writing a 20-page essay, a book, or a business plan.

A more effective approach is to break down larger content into smaller pieces and work on each piece individually with ChatGPT; chunking. First, divide the larger content into smaller sections. Then, break each of these sections down into even smaller pieces. With many smaller pieces at your disposal, you can use ChatGPT to work on them piece by piece. Keep a separate document open to copy and paste each of these pieces into, gradually building up the larger whole.

By following this process, you can get around ChatGPT's output limitations and work on larger projects without overwhelming the AI or the servers at OpenAI.

Let's say I have an idea for creating tailor-made outfits for cats. To turn this idea into a full business plan, I can start by asking ChatGPT to create an outline for me. I can give it a general overview of my idea and ask it to come up with a structured plan to help me turn this dream into reality.

I have an idea for creating tailor-made outfits for cats. Create the outline of a business plan for this idea

 Sure! Here is a basic outline for a business plan for a company that creates tailor-made outfits for cats:

Executive Summary:

- Introduce the company and its mission to create high-quality, fashionable, and comfortable outfits for cats.
- Outline the unique selling points of the company (e.g., custom-fit designs, wide range of styles and fabrics to choose from, etc.).

Market Analysis:

- Research and analyze the target market for cat owners who are interested in buying outfits for their pets.
- Identify key competitors and how the company's products and services differ from those of the competition.

Product and Services:

- Describe the types of outfits that the company will offer (e.g., sweaters, raincoats, Halloween costumes, etc.).
- Explain the process for customers to order custom-fit outfits, including options for selecting fabrics and styles.

Marketing and Sales:

- Outline the marketing strategy for reaching potential customers, such as through social media, partnerships with pet stores, or participation in cat shows and events.
- Discuss pricing and how the company will handle sales (e.g., online store, wholesale to retailers).

(ChatGPT's outline had 3 extra sections. Our example won't need them)

As you can see, ChatGPT gave us a high-level outline for this business plan, including key areas like market analysis and financial projections. However, this outline is still quite broad and might be overwhelming to work with all at once. That's why it can be helpful to break it down into even smaller chunks.

For example, let's say I want to focus on just the first section of the outline: "Market Analysis." I can ask ChatGPT to help me break this section down into more manageable chunks.

Break down the market analysis into sub sections, base this on my idea

 Sure! Here are some potential sub-sections that could be included in the market analysis section of a business plan for a company that creates tailor-made outfits for cats:

- Target market: Describe the demographic of cat owners who are most likely to be interested in purchasing outfits for their pets. This could include factors such as age, income, location, and lifestyle.
- Market size: Estimate the size of the market for cat outfits, including the number of cat owners in the target demographic and their potential spending on this type of product.
- Market trends: Research and discuss any trends or changes in the market that could impact the demand for cat outfits. For example, are more people interested in dressing up their pets now compared to the past? Is there a trend towards more natural or sustainable materials for pet products?
- Competition: Identify and analyze key competitors in the market, including their products, pricing, marketing strategies, and target customer demographic.
- Market needs: Identify any unmet needs or gaps in the market that the company's products could address. For example, is there a lack of high-quality, custom-fit cat outfits available? Are there few options for cats with unique body shapes or sizes?
- Marketing and sales channels: Research and discuss the most effective channels for reaching potential customers and making sales. This could include online marketplaces, physical retail stores, social media, or partnerships with pet stores or other businesses.

Now, instead of trying to tackle the entire market analysis section at once, I can work on these smaller pieces one by one. And once I have completed each of these sub-sections, I can copy and paste them into a word processor to create the full market analysis section of my business plan. By following this process for each main category of my business plan, I can use ChatGPT to create a comprehensive, well-organised document that covers all the key aspects of my business idea.

Think of it as divide, divide, and conquer. Break up anything large you have into smaller pieces, either by asking ChatGPT to do it or by doing that yourself, then keep dividing the sub-chunks until the portions are small enough for ChatGPT to handle.

Here are some thoughts to help you better choose what size each of these portions should be. There is a trade-off between long output and short output. If you divide down the text into many many many smaller parts, you need to pay more attention to make sure that there is a consistency of language style; imagine one paragraph being casual and the next using academic jargon. However the longer each of ChatGPT's outputs are the more difficult it is for you to pinpoint your feedback and to shape the text using an iterative process.

This means that there is no one-size-fits-all when it comes to dividing larger content into smaller pieces, instead I recommend exploring different approaches while completing the exercises, and finding an answer that works for you.

Your turn to **create some lengthy content with the chunking approach**

Writing lengthy content takes time and energy from both you and ChatGPT. So this exercise is divided into two attempts: a first straight forward divide, divide, and conquer approach, and a second more thought out approach. I recommend that you complete these two in order to get the most out of this learning process.

Writing a Play - First Attempt

Use ChatGPT to help you write a play. Start by brainstorming an idea or seeking inspiration from your AI friend. Once you have your concept, break it down into smaller components by asking ChatGPT to divide the play into acts, and then each act into scenes. After outlining each scene, ask ChatGPT to write the dialogue for Scene 1 of Act 1. Make sure to ask ChatGPT to include specific acting notes and vivid visual descriptions of the setting to bring the scene to life

This cat has been strategically placed to prevent you from seeing the instructions of the second attempt before you complete this first step.

Writing a Play - Second Attempt

This time, let's start by taking advantage of ChatGPT's contextual understanding to build out the world within your play. For this attempt, create a new chat by clicking 'New Chat' on the top left of your screen. Start by discussing your idea for a play with ChatGPT, then ask it to build a set of characters. For each of these characters, use our iterative process to develop them the way you see fit (check out the chapter on 'Iteration for Excellence' for a refresher). Once you have all of your characters, go ahead and pick a city or country for the setting, ask ChatGPT to make up some recent events, and take your time to develop the universe of your play.

Now that we have our characters and setting, we can repeat the process from before to make an outline of all the acts and scenes and write the dialogue for Act 1, Scene 1.

Use this space to write down your thoughts, tips & tricks!

PART III
ADVANCED PROMPT ENGINEERING

THE SKY IS NOT THE LIMIT

IT'S JUST THE VIEW

10

CO-CREATION

ChatGPT is capable of creating excellent content if you guide it correctly. All the techniques covered in this book, including a conversational approach, roleplay, training ChatGPT, and chunking, can be used to transform ChatGPT into your perfect ghostwriter. With just these tools and techniques alone, you can significantly decrease the time required for administrative tasks and content creation. Instead of doing the work yourself, you can learn to direct ChatGPT to meet your expectations.

This chapter takes a different approach. Instead of focusing on how to get ChatGPT to write or create something for you, let's explore how it can help and guide you to create something incredible.

Imagine ChatGPT as a futuristic car; you can either put it on autopilot and let it do an excellent job or use the technology to guide your driving and together create a more powerful experience.

Currently, I am writing a new book called 'The True Cost of ChatGPT on Humanity, Languages, and Inequality.' It is a much darker narrative about the impact of ChatGPT than what you may be used to reading from me. I will be using this co-creation approach when writing it. Therefore, for our use case, let's see how I would write a chapter of the book.

Use ChatGPT to Think

When creating something, your first step is usually internal; considering the ideas, structure, message, or impact of what you will be working on.

During my university days, I used to claim that most of my essays and papers were conceptualised in the pub. Not physically, but all the ideas, explanations, counterarguments, and different perspectives emerged from discussions with others. Because my mind was focused on my topic, it would frequently come up in conversations, and others would inadvertently become part of my writing process.

It was not the pub itself that helped me, but the ability to bounce ideas off another person. Not everyone has a group of individuals who are willing to engage in nuanced or technical discussions about their work, which is where ChatGPT can assist.

Let's apply this to a chapter in my book. The chapter I will be focusing on is about how ChatGPT's architecture favours English over other languages, which I will call 'The Token Problem.' Instead of explaining the concept to you, I will use ChatGPT to help me consider it.

Act as a software architect who has worked on OpenAI's ChatGPT. I will ask you questions about the architecture and how different languages are processed differently, and you will give me in-depth explanations, using analogies and accessible language, but also giving me the key technical terms.

My first question is why does the same text in English cost less tokens than in Hindi or Ukrainian

 Great question! The reason why the same text in English costs less tokens than in Hindi or Ukrainian has to do with the fundamental differences in the structure and complexity of these languages.

In natural language processing (NLP), a token is the basic unit of text processing. It is essentially a sequence of characters that represents a single meaningful element of the language, such as a word, punctuation mark, or number.

English is a relatively simple language in terms of its grammar and syntax. It has a relatively small number of verb tenses and noun declensions, and its word order is fairly straightforward. This means that English words can often be represented by a single token, whereas in more complex languages like Hindi or Ukrainian, a single word might require multiple tokens to capture its various inflections and suffixes.

For example, in English, the word "cat" would be represented by a single token, but in Hindi, the word "billi" (which also means "cat") would require two tokens: "billi" and "ਿੋ" (the symbol represents a vowel modifier).

This increased complexity means that the same text in Hindi or Ukrainian will require more tokens than the equivalent text in English. This is because the NLP model needs to capture more information about each word in order to accurately understand its meaning and context.

To put it simply, imagine that you are trying to build a puzzle. In English, the puzzle pieces are relatively simple and fit together easily. But in Hindi or Ukrainian, the puzzle pieces are more complex and have many more interlocking parts, which makes them more difficult and time-consuming to put together. Similarly, in NLP, the more complex structure of Hindi or Ukrainian requires more tokens to represent the same text as in English, which increases the computational cost of processing that text.

Instead of considering the output as text that I can use directly in my book, I see it as the beginning of a conversation where I can ask more questions. Some follow-up questions I might ask are:

- Apart from grammar, what are other reasons for the difference in token costs?
- What is the role of different alphabets?
- How can we level the playing field between these languages?
- I believe that inequality in token costs could lead to inequality in digital inclusion because developers prefer languages with lower training and usage costs. What do you think?
- What are the real-world impacts of languages having vastly different token costs?

My goal is not to get ChatGPT to write text for me but to use it to help me organise my thoughts. I can steer the direction of our conversation, and it can assist me in developing any opinions or arguments that I want to include in my book. Using ChatGPT to aid in thinking instead of writing can be a valuable first step on your co-creation journey.

Rather than changing the text, it can be more powerful, albeit more time-consuming, to ask ChatGPT for feedback and guidance.

Let's assume that after my conversation with ChatGPT about languages and tokens, I have a section of my chapter that is almost ready to go into my book. Using the techniques discussed in the previous section, we could:

- Use a conversational approach to improve the writing style, language, and flow of the text.
- Ask ChatGPT to take on the persona of a particular author and rewrite the text in their voice.
- Train ChatGPT on our writing style and ask it to apply it to the text.

However, each of these approaches puts ChatGPT in the driver's seat. In this chapter, we want to use ChatGPT's technology to improve the way we write, not just the text itself. We could ask ChatGPT to provide feedback and suggestions to help us improve our own work.

To use more of our tools, I could ask ChatGPT to take on the role of a newspaper editor or a book publisher to set expectations for the feedback I'm seeking.

Act as an editor from a known publishing house. I am an author working on a book that we will soon release. Please provide me with critical feedback in bullet point format on the following text to ensure that it meets your publishing house's high standards:

"ChatGPT divides its processing costs in unites of tokens, however the number of these tokens isn't equal across languages. When ChatGPT receives an input, it needs to break it down into more understandable chunks of information. This is a bit like what we do with breaking down books into chapters, then into paragraphs, then into sentences, then into words, and then into syllables, then into letters. We don't ask someone to absorb a book all at once, instead this happens after they have gone through all the words on the pages and made sense of what they meant when brought together."

 Overall Feedback:

- The text could benefit from some restructuring to make it more concise and coherent.
- Consider defining some technical terms to ensure clarity for the reader.
- There are also a few grammatical errors that should be addressed.

Specific Feedback:

- Consider rephrasing the first sentence for clarity: "ChatGPT's processing costs are divided into units of tokens, but the number of tokens varies across languages."
- Define "tokens" and "input" for the reader's understanding.
- The analogy used to explain breaking down information is helpful, but it could be streamlined to avoid redundancy. Consider combining some of the steps (e.g., "breaking down books into chapters and paragraphs").
- Change "This is a bit like" to "This process is similar to" for clarity.
- Consider rephrasing "We don't ask someone to absorb a book all at once" to "Readers are not expected to absorb a book all at once."
- Change "instead this happens" to "rather, this process occurs" for clarity.
- Address the grammatical errors:
    - "break it down" instead of "break down"
    - "units" instead of "unites"
    - "syllables and letters" instead of "syllables, then into letters"

We can then use a conversational approach to work on the feedback together. My aim is not to ask ChatGPT to implement the feedback but to engage in a discussion that will allow me to implement the feedback in a better way.

I can train ChatGPT by providing it with examples of the type of writing I would like my work to aspire to. This will help ChatGPT provide the feedback I'm seeking. (I've slightly cut out part of my prompt to make sure it fits on this page)

Here is an example of a writing style that I like. Analyse this text, and then give me feedback on how I can improve my previous text with this in mind.

"I have been intending to write this essay for months. Why am I finally doing it? Because I finally found some uncommitted time? Wrong. I have papers to grade, textbook orders to fill out, an NSF proposal to referee, dissertation drafts to read. I am working on this essay as a way of not doing all of those things. This is the essence of what I call structured procrastination, an amazing strategy I have discovered that converts procrastinators into effective human beings, respected and admired for all that they can accomplish and the good use they make of time. All procrastinators put off things they have to do. Structured procrastination is the art of making this bad trait work for you.

 Analysis:

The writer uses a conversational and engaging tone, which draws the reader in and keeps them interested. They also use humor to make their point, which helps to make the text more relatable and memorable. The text is well-organized, with clear transitions between ideas and a strong thesis statement.

The writer also uses concrete examples and anecdotes to support their argument, which helps to make their points more convincing. They also use repetition to emphasize their main ideas and create a sense of rhythm in the text.

Improvement Suggestions:

- Consider using a more conversational and engaging tone in your text, like the author of the example text. This will help to make your writing more relatable and interesting to readers.
- Use concrete examples and anecdotes to support your argument, as the author of the example text does. This will make your points more convincing and memorable.
- Use repetition to emphasize your main ideas, as the author of the example text does. This will create a sense of rhythm in your writing and help your ideas to stick in the reader's mind.
- Be sure to organize your text effectively, with clear transitions between ideas and a strong thesis statement. This will make it easier for readers to follow your argument and understand your main points.

Exercises

Throughout this chapter, we have been using the power of ChatGPT without asking it to do the work for us. Instead of simply directing ChatGPT, we are using its assistance to help us achieve our goals. Try these exercises to see the difference for yourself.

- What challenges would a family face if they wanted to move to Mars?
- What would society look like on Mars if there were less than 50 people there?
- Here is my sci-fi book idea about two families moving to Mars: "your idea." Can you provide feedback on how I could improve it? Use a conversational approach, going back and forth, to help you develop your idea.

Now, start a different chat and ask ChatGPT the following:
"Create an outline for a science fiction book about two families who are among the first settlers on Mars."

Compare the differences between ChatGPT's outline and the idea you had ChatGPT help you develop.

Use this space to write down your thoughts, tips & tricks!

11

[FORMAT] YOUR OUTPUT

Once you've mastered the basics of ChatGPT, and you're ready to take more control of your output, learning how to format your responses can take your prompt engineering to the next level. If you've just started your ChatGPT journey and haven't completed the exercises in the other chapters yet, I highly recommend coming back to this chapter after you've had a bit more practice, as you'll be able to get so much more out of it.

When you give ChatGPT a prompt, you can suggest what kind of format or structure it should use when creating its output. For instance, when asking it to write a poem, you could request 6-line stanzas or ask it to rhyme or be an acrostic. When writing an essay, you could ask for 4 paragraphs and provide more information about what you'd like in each paragraph, as well as subheaders for each one.

However, ChatGPT doesn't always follow your formatting and structuring requests, especially when you give multiple requests in the same prompt. Additionally, because it can be a complex process to tell ChatGPT exactly how to format the output, most people don't tend to bother with it.

If you learn to use formatting correctly, you'll never look at ChatGPT the same way again. So, let's find out how this works.

When ChatGPT sees square brackets [], it knows that this is a placeholder for information. OpenAI calls this [insert], but we'll use the term [format] to make learning about this technique easier.

For example, if you give the prompt: "There is a [animal] by the lake", ChatGPT will fill in the placeholder with an animal name, effectively creating a prompt within the prompt, or prompt-ception.

Once upon a time there was a [animal] by the lake

 Once upon a time there was a swan by the lake. The swan lived in a peaceful, serene environment surrounded by the calming waters of the lake. It spent its days gliding gracefully across the surface of the water, searching for small fish and plants to eat.

The other animals in the area admired the swan's beauty and elegance. They would often gather around the lake to watch it swim and listen to its soothing song. The swan, however, preferred to keep to itself most of the time, enjoying the tranquility of its surroundings.

One day, a group of mischievous ducks arrived at the lake. They saw the swan and decided to play a prank on it. They started making loud noises and splashing water all around, trying to disrupt the swan's peaceful routine.

The swan, at first, was startled by the sudden commotion. But then it realized what was happening and decided to ignore the ducks. It continued to glide across the water, unperturbed by their antics.

The ducks, frustrated by their failed attempt to bother the swan, eventually gave up and swam away. The swan was left to enjoy the peacefulness of the lake once again.

From that day on, the swan became even more admired by the other animals for its calm and serene demeanor. And the ducks learned to appreciate the beauty of the lake in their own way, without disturbing its peaceful inhabitants.

But, as you can see, if left to its own devices, ChatGPT can go rogue and revert back to its autocompletion self. So, we need to consider how to use the [format] correctly.

Framing / Templates

Let's explore a more complex example so we can begin to appreciate the true power of formatting. In this next example, I will ask ChatGPT to help me write a story, but instead of just providing the context, I will build a frame and let ChatGPT fill in the rest.

> [Name] was [verb] [adverb] [adjective] to [city] when [something very unexpected happened]. [Name of character's friend] [what that person said]. [The reaction of our main character, which was taken badly by their friend].

 Samantha was driving anxiously to New York City when her car suddenly broke down in the middle of nowhere. "I told you we should have taken my car," her friend Alex said, annoyed. Samantha sighed heavily and snapped, "Well, we didn't, so what's the point of talking about it now?" Alex's expression turned sour at Samantha's response, clearly hurt by her friend's tone.

Realizing her mistake, Samantha quickly apologized and explained that she was just stressed about the car troubles. Alex reluctantly forgave her, but the tension between them remained for the rest of the journey. Samantha couldn't help but feel guilty about her outburst and resolved to make it up to Alex during their trip to the city.

In this example, I used three different types of formatting prompts:

- One-word descriptions (name, city, etc.)
- Word types (verb, adverb, adjective, etc.)
- Prompts (something very unexpected happened...)

I call this approach formatting framing because it requires us to rethink how we write our prompts. We need to understand how we want to frame the output and then give specific instructions for each element.

Aside from using formatting for framing, it's also very useful for defining the structure of ChatGPT's output. For instance, if we wanted ChatGPT to write a blog post about why turtles may one day rule the world, we can use [formatting] to ensure that the output structure follows the format we want for our blog post.

Write a blog post about how turtles may one day take over the world, using accessible language and an over enthusiastic tone, in the following format:

"[catchy title that uses a pun]
[hook about the consequences of turtles taking over the world]
[unrealistic question about turtles]
[paragraph developing a clever answer to the question. Making up some facts, but making them sound true]
[hook that questions our current knowledge about nature]
[paragraph about how nature conspires against us, using 2 different examples and developing them]
[continued discussion of nature's conspiracy but now applied to turtles and their dominating instincts]
[concluding paragraph that confuses the reader]
[cliff hanger]"

Head to the next page to see what ChatGPT was able to output with this prompt.

By using formatting, you can gain much more control over the structure and flow of the content while still leveraging ChatGPT to do the heavy lifting. I highly recommend using formatting to create a more polished first draft, and then moving on to a conversational approach to refine the output. This can help you to achieve a balance between structure and creativity, allowing you to make the most out of your ChatGPT interactions.

Have you ever imagined a world where turtles rule the land, the sea, and the air? Where our slow and steady friends take control of every aspect of our lives? It might sound like a silly idea, but what if it wasn't?

Could turtles really take over the world? Well, let's take a look at some interesting facts. Did you know that turtles have been around for over 200 million years? That means they've outlasted dinosaurs and countless other species. And did you know that turtles are incredibly adaptable creatures? They can survive in a wide range of environments, from tropical forests to freezing tundras. These two facts alone suggest that turtles might have some secret abilities that we're not aware of.

But wait, could nature really be conspiring against us? It's a crazy idea, but if you think about it, there are plenty of examples. Take mosquitoes, for instance. They seem to exist solely to annoy us with their constant buzzing and biting. Or what about poison ivy? It's like nature said, "Hey, let's create a plant that will make people miserable for days!" So maybe, just maybe, nature has a plan that we don't know about.

Now, let's apply this concept to turtles. They might seem harmless and cute, but what if they have a hidden agenda? What if they've been biding their time, waiting for the perfect moment to strike? Think about it, turtles have some pretty impressive qualities. They're incredibly patient, they have a tough outer shell that can protect them from almost anything, and some species can live for over 100 years. It's not hard to imagine a scenario where turtles use these abilities to their advantage and take over the world.

Now, let's apply this concept to turtles. They might seem harmless and cute, but what if they have a hidden agenda? What if they've been biding their time, waiting for the perfect moment to strike? Think about it, turtles have some pretty impressive qualities. They're incredibly patient, they have a tough outer shell that can protect them from almost anything, and some species can live for over 100 years. It's not hard to imagine a scenario where turtles use these abilities to their advantage and take over the world.

So, what does the future hold? Will turtles really take over the world? It's hard to say for sure, but one thing is certain - nature always finds a way. Whether it's through mosquitoes, poison ivy, or even turtles, the natural world has a way of surprising us. Maybe we should keep a closer eye on those turtles after all...

Will we be living in a turtle-ruled world in the near future? Only time will tell. But one thing's for sure - we should always be ready for the unexpected. Who knows what other surprises nature has in store for us? Stay tuned, folks, because the future is anyone's guess!

Next Level: text to template to text

If you already have an example of the type of output you are looking for, then you can use a text-to-template-to-text workflow to elevate your content creation.

Here is how it works: Suppose you have a sales email that performed exceptionally well or a newspaper article that gained unexpected traction. Using ChatGPT, you can create a template format from that example and then utilise it to structure future content.

Analyse the structure of this text. Replace each part of the text with [] creating a template that could be used for any sales email.

"Subject Line: Protect Your Turtle's Shell with Shell Shine

Dear [Recipient],

I hope this email finds you well. As a fellow turtle lover, I wanted to share with you a product that I have found to be incredibly helpful in protecting my pet's shell.

Shell Shine is an all-natural product designed to protect and restore your turtle's shell, keeping it strong and healthy for years to come. Our formula is gentle and safe for your pet, and it helps to protect against damage such as scratches and cracks.

Not only does Shell Shine protect your turtle's shell, but it also helps to restore its natural shine and luster. Our unique formula brings out the natural colors in your turtle's shell, making it look as beautiful as it did when your pet was just a hatchling.

If you're interested in trying out Shell Shine, we offer a 100% satisfaction guarantee. Simply apply a small amount of the product to your turtle's shell, and watch it shine like never before.

Thank you for considering Shell Shine as a way to protect and restore your turtle's shell. We believe that you and your pet will be thrilled with the results.

Best regards,

Turtle Shine Ltd."

[Subject Line: Briefly summarize the product or service being offered]

Dear [Recipient],

[Opening sentence that shows empathy or personal connection with the recipient]

[Introduce the product or service and its benefits. Highlight the unique features and how it solves the recipient's problem or meets their needs]

[Explain how the product or service works, and why it is effective. Use facts, statistics or testimonials to build credibility]

[Provide a call to action, urging the recipient to take action. Offer a guarantee or a free trial to increase the likelihood of a purchase]

[Thank the recipient for considering the product or service, and express confidence that they will be satisfied with the results]

[Closing sentence that shows appreciation and encourages a response]

Best regards,

[Your Name or Company Name]

This process allows us to transform from text to a template. The following step is to use the created template and follow the steps outlined in the "Output Formatting" section to produce new text using the same structure as the original input. This allows us to reproduce the success of the original piece and generate similar content with the same impact.

Head over to the next page to see how we can use this template to write a new sales email about a different product or campaign.

Credit for this idea goes to Randy Zales, who came up with it during one of our training sessions. Ideas like this ensure that every training session I conduct is an opportunity for me to learn more and share more with you in this book.

Use this template to write a sales email about a new coffee beans product. These beans are hand picked, hand roasted, and don't taste like turtles.

Subject Line: Enjoy Premium Coffee with Our Hand-Picked and Hand-Roasted Beans

Dear [Recipient],

Do you love the taste of coffee but want to try something new and unique? Our new coffee beans are hand-picked, hand-roasted, and guaranteed not to taste like turtles.

We understand that coffee lovers like you appreciate the finest quality coffee that has been carefully prepared to perfection. That's why we are excited to introduce our new coffee beans, which are hand-picked and hand-roasted by our expert roasters to ensure the freshest and most delicious coffee you've ever tasted.

Our coffee beans are grown in the finest coffee plantations around the world, and we only select the best quality beans for our customers. We carefully roast each bean in small batches, to bring out the unique flavors and aromas of each origin.

Our coffee beans are perfect for anyone who wants to enjoy premium coffee with a rich and smooth taste. Whether you prefer a classic espresso or a creamy latte, our beans will deliver a unique and satisfying coffee experience.

To ensure your complete satisfaction, we offer a 100% money-back guarantee. If for any reason you are not completely satisfied with our coffee beans, we will refund your purchase.

Thank you for considering our new coffee beans as your next coffee experience. We look forward to providing you with the finest quality coffee you deserve.

Best regards,

[Your Name or Company Name]

Exercises

Now it's your turn to take control by [formatting] your output. Here are three exercises to help you practice:

Generate full contact information for five random people using [formatting] prompts.
Ask ChatGPT to create the contact details exactly the way you want them to be.

Create a sales email template that uses [formatting] prompts to reach out to leads and gauge their interest in your service.
Once you have the template, use it to create three different emails for three different services.

Take a piece of text from any online source and replace a sentence with a new prompt using [formatting].

Use this space to write down your thoughts, tips & tricks!

12

BUILDING PERSONAS

Adopting a design thinking approach and focusing on users is essential in today's fast-paced world. By putting users at the heart of the design process, we can truly understand what they need and want. For instance, when creating a mobile app, knowing the user's needs leads to a more enjoyable and easy-to-use experience. In healthcare, focusing on users can result in treatments that are easier to access and better suited for patients with different needs. Sometimes, we can be so caught up in our own perspectives that we might not see what others need.

Now, let's explore how we can use ChatGPT to tap into the power of this user-focused model with personas.

In this chapter, we're going to look at a situation where we're writing a company newsletter about adapting to AI tools.

To use a user-focused approach for this scenario, we should start by figuring out who will be reading our content and create mini profiles for each type of person. Doing this helps us understand their needs better and create content that connects with everyone.

Here's an example of a prompt we could give ChatGPT to help us create various personas for our company newsletter:

ChatGPT, can you help me come up with 3 different personas for our internal company newsletter about getting used to AI tools? Our company specializes in marketing and has a diverse workforce, including creative designers, content writers, marketing strategists, and data analysts. Please consider different roles within the organization, their varying levels of technical expertise, and their unique concerns and interests when it comes to using AI. Give me a short description for each persona, including their job title, background, and main interests or concerns about integrating AI into their daily work.

Sure, I can definitely help you with that! Here are three different personas for your internal company newsletter about getting used to AI tools:

1. Creative Designer - "Sarah"

Job title: Senior Graphic Designer

Background: Sarah has been working as a graphic designer for over 10 years and has a wealth of experience in creating visually stunning designs for various marketing campaigns. She has always been interested in the latest design trends and enjoys experimenting with different styles and techniques.

Interests/Concerns: Sarah is excited about the prospect of using AI tools to improve her designs and streamline her workflow. However, she is also worried that relying too much on these tools might stifle her creativity or result in a decrease in the quality of her work. She is looking for tips and best practices for integrating AI tools into her creative process without sacrificing her artistic vision.

2. Content Writer - "Alex"

Job title: Content Marketing Manager

Background: Alex has been working in content marketing for several years and is responsible for creating engaging and informative content for various channels such as blogs, social media, and email campaigns. She is skilled at crafting compelling stories and has a keen eye for detail.

Interests/Concerns: Alex is interested in using AI tools to improve the effectiveness of her content and to gain insights into what resonates with her target audience. However, she is also worried about the potential for AI-generated content to come across as robotic or impersonal. She is looking for guidance on how to strike the right balance between human creativity and AI-powered optimization.

3. Data Analyst - "Tom"

Job title: Senior Marketing Analyst

Background: Tom has a background in statistics and is responsible for analyzing and interpreting data to inform marketing strategy. He is skilled at using tools such as Excel and SQL to manipulate and visualize data.

Interests/Concerns: Tom is interested in using AI tools to help him automate repetitive tasks and to gain deeper insights into complex datasets. However, he is also worried about the accuracy and reliability of these tools and wants to ensure that the data he is using to make decisions is trustworthy. He is looking for information on the latest AI-powered data analysis techniques and best practices for validating and interpreting AI-generated insights.

ChatGPT has provided us with three well-defined personas that cater to our diverse workforce: Sarah the Creative Designer, Alex the Content Writer, and Tom the Data Analyst. Each persona has unique interests, concerns, and backgrounds that are relevant to our user-centric approach. This allows us to tailor our content to address their individual needs and expectations, ultimately making our newsletter more engaging and relevant to our readers.

Now that we have our personas, let's move on to using them effectively.

Using Personas for Ideation

Before we start writing our content, it's important to think about what each persona would want to get out of the newsletter, the format it should be in, and the language we should use. By doing this, we can ensure that our content is tailored to our audience and resonates with each reader.

Let's explore how we can work with ChatGPT to consider the needs of each persona when creating our newsletter.

First, we can use the personas to brainstorm what kind of information and insights each reader might be looking for in the newsletter. For example, Sarah might be interested in learning about new AI design tools, while Alex might want to know how to create engaging content using AI, and Tom could be curious about AI-powered data analysis techniques.

Here's an example of a prompt we could write for ChatGPT, to help us brainstorm some ideas for our newsletter.

> *ChatGPT, please help me brainstorm ideas for our internal company newsletter about adapting to AI tools, keeping in mind the interests of our three personas:*
> (Personas)

Sure, here are some ideas for your internal company newsletter that cater to the interests and concerns of your three personas:

For Sarah, the Creative Designer:

1. Showcase successful case studies of designers who have integrated AI tools into their creative process while still maintaining their artistic vision.
2. Share tips and best practices on how to use AI tools as a starting point for creative inspiration, rather than a replacement for human creativity.
3. Provide training resources or workshops that demonstrate how to use AI tools in a way that complements and enhances creative skills.
4. Highlight the benefits of using AI tools, such as increased productivity, more accurate measurements of performance metrics, and freeing up time to focus on more challenging design tasks.

Format: A combination of written articles and visual examples, such as infographics or video tutorials, would be an effective format for Sarah. The language should be accessible and not overly technical, with a focus on real-world examples and actionable advice.

2. Content Writer - "Alex"

Job title: Content Marketing Manager

Background: Alex has been working in content marketing for several years and is responsible for creating engaging and informative content for various channels such as blogs, social media, and email campaigns. She is skilled at crafting compelling stories and has a keen eye for detail.

Interests/Concerns: Alex is interested in using AI tools to improve the effectiveness of her content and to gain insights into what resonates with her target audience. However, she is also worried about the potential for AI-generated content to come across as robotic or impersonal. She is looking for guidance on how to strike the right balance between human creativity and AI-powered optimization.

3. Data Analyst - "Tom"

Job title: Senior Marketing Analyst

Background: Tom has a background in statistics and is responsible for analyzing and interpreting data to inform marketing strategy. He is skilled at using tools such as Excel and SQL to manipulate and visualize data.

Interests/Concerns: Tom is interested in using AI tools to help him automate repetitive tasks and to gain deeper insights into complex datasets. However, he is also worried about the accuracy and reliability of these tools and wants to ensure that the data he is using to make decisions is trustworthy. He is looking for information on the latest AI-powered data analysis techniques and best practices for validating and interpreting AI-generated insights.

We've received a range of ideas from ChatGPT for our internal company newsletter, focusing on the unique interests and concerns of our three personas: Sarah the Creative Designer, Alex the Content Writer, and Tom the Data Analyst. By addressing each persona's specific needs, we can create engaging and relevant content that truly connects with our audience.

In the output, ChatGPT also considers the best formats and language styles for every persona, ensuring that we're speaking their language and presenting information in the most accessible way. For example, Sarah would appreciate visual examples and straightforward language, while Tom would find more technical language with a focus on practical applications appealing. By taking these preferences into account, we can craft a newsletter that's not only informative but enjoyable for everyone.

Using personas to get feedback on our work.

Just like focus groups, which gather people together to discuss their opinions and reactions to a product or idea, we can use our personas to help ChatGPT give specific feedback on our content. Focus groups are great for understanding how different people might perceive and interact with something, allowing us to make improvements based on their thoughts and feelings.

By giving ChatGPT our personas and the content we've made, we can get feedback that takes into account the unique needs and preferences of each persona. This helps us understand how different people might see our content and make changes to improve it, similar to gathering insights from a focus group.

There's a small challenge with ChatGPT – it has a character limit for each interaction. To work around this issue, we can communicate with ChatGPT in two parts. First, we'll give ChatGPT our newsletter draft using this prompt:

> *Here's the current draft of our company's newsletter. We want to use a user-centric approach when improving the newsletter.*
> *I will start by giving you the newsletter and you will ask me for the personas, so you can give user-specific feedback.*
> *(Newsletter)*

This forces ChatGPT to automatically move onto our personas. If we just gave ChatGPT the newsletter, it might try to summarise it, feedback it, or go rouge in another way.

 Thanks for sharing the newsletter draft. Can you please provide me with the personas of the employees who will be receiving this newsletter? This will help me tailor my feedback to their specific needs and concerns.

After getting this response from ChatGPT, we can then give the personas for user-specific feedback. For our use case, this is what ChatGPT replied:

 Thank you for providing the personas of the employees who will be receiving this newsletter. Here are some user-centric feedback based on the interests and concerns of each persona:

- For Sarah, as a Senior Graphic Designer, it would be helpful to provide more specific examples of how AI tools can enhance rather than replace creativity. You can emphasize that AI can automate repetitive tasks such as resizing and retouching images, allowing designers like Sarah to focus on more high-value work such as concept creation and ideation. Also, providing some tips on how Sarah can integrate AI tools into her creative process without sacrificing her artistic vision would be useful.
- For Alex, as a Content Marketing Manager, it would be helpful to reassure her that AI-generated content can be customized to reflect the brand's unique voice and tone. You can also emphasize that AI tools can assist her in generating data-driven insights to inform her content creation strategies, allowing her to produce content that resonates better with her target audience. It would be useful to provide examples of how other companies have successfully integrated AI tools into their content marketing strategies while maintaining a human touch.
- For Tom, as a Senior Marketing Analyst, it would be helpful to provide more information on the specific AI-powered data analysis techniques that can be used to gain deeper insights into complex datasets. It would also be helpful to provide tips on how Tom can validate and interpret AI-generated insights to ensure that the data he is using to make decisions is trustworthy. You can also emphasize that AI tools can help Tom automate time-consuming tasks such as data cleaning and preparation, allowing him to spend more time on analysis and interpretation.

By using this two-step approach, we can get feedback from ChatGPT that considers the interests and concerns of our diverse audience, similar to collecting insights from a focus group. This helps us improve our content and make it more appealing and effective for everyone.

Exercise

Ready to put your newfound knowledge of personas to practical use? This exercise will guide you through the process of creating personas with ChatGPT, tailoring content to their unique needs and interests, and refining your work based on feedback. This hands-on approach will help you truly understand the power of personas in content creation. Let's dive in!

1) Crafting Personas

Imagine you are creating a blog post about the future of renewable energy. Use ChatGPT to help you create at least three different personas that would be interested in your blog post. Consider factors such as their jobs, their interests, and why they would be reading your post.

2) Tailoring Content

For each persona, brainstorm what kind of information they would be looking for in the blog post. What format should this information be in? What language should you use? Write down your ideas for each persona.

3) Working with ChatGPT

Interact with ChatGPT to brainstorm ideas for your blog post tailored to each persona. Remember to consider the unique interests and concerns of each persona.

4) Review and Reflect

Compare the ideas you brainstormed with the suggestions provided by ChatGPT. Do they align? Are there any new insights or ideas you gained from ChatGPT's suggestions?

5) Creating Content and Getting Feedback

Draft a section of your blog post for one of your personas. Ask ChatGPT for feedback, specifying the persona for which the content is intended. Reflect on the feedback you received. How does it align with the needs and preferences of your persona? What improvements can you make?

6) Iterate and Refine

Apply the feedback from ChatGPT to refine your draft. Repeat this process for all your personas until you have a blog post that caters to each of your reader's interests and concerns.

Use this space to write down your thoughts, tips & tricks!

13

CHAIN PROMPTING

As we have seen throughout this book, ChatGPT is a fantastic AI language model that helps generate human-like responses to prompts and questions. But remember that it works by guessing the next best word based on the context. While this is useful for many tasks, sometimes it can struggle with more complex problems that need a deeper understanding or a more organised approach.

Imagine solving a tough maths equation. Trying to jump straight to the answer can be confusing and often leads to errors. Instead, we break the problem into smaller, easier-to-handle steps and work our way through each one to get the solution. This step-by-step approach can also be applied to ChatGPT, making it more effective at tackling complex tasks and generating better outputs.

This is where the idea of Chain Prompting comes in. Think of a chain made up of many links, with each one connecting directly to the next. With ChatGPT, we can create a specific workflow that includes a series of prompts or questions. The AI then uses the output from each step as the basis for the next one. This method lets ChatGPT build momentum and work through larger or more complex workloads step by step.

Chain Prompting helps users guide ChatGPT through a process that slowly refines the output. By breaking complex tasks into smaller steps, the AI can generate more specific, customised, and overall better results. This approach is really useful for creating content, like articles or blog posts, where having a structured outline is key for making the content easy to read and follow.

One practical use case for Chain Prompting is writing a blog post that performs well in terms of SEO (Search Engine Optimisation). SEO is the practice of optimising your website's content, so search engines like Google are more likely to rank it higher in search results. For a blog post, good SEO means increased visibility, more organic traffic, and ultimately, higher chances of reaching your target audience.

In our case, the primary goal is to create a blog post that ranks well in search results, rather than focusing solely on the content itself. This means we need to consider the various elements that contribute to SEO performance, like keywords, headlines, and structure, when crafting our blog post.

To start, we need to think about the step-by-step process that we would follow if we were to write a high-performing SEO blog post. The first few steps would include identifying common questions related to the topic, generating a list of popular keywords and phrases, choosing the most relevant questions and keywords for the headline and subheadings, and creating an outline for the post.

Once we have a clear idea of the steps involved, we can then turn each step into a prompt for ChatGPT. This can be done manually or by asking ChatGPT to build the prompts for us. In doing so, we create a chain prompt that guides ChatGPT through the entire process of crafting a high-SEO-performing blog post.

Here's an example of a 10-step chain prompt for writing a blog post with great SEO performance:

1) ChatGPT, please provide a list of common questions related to [Topic].

2) Based on the provided list of questions, let's generate a list of popular keywords and phrases associated with [Topic], focusing on high search volume and low competition.

3) From the list of common questions and keywords, please choose the most relevant ones and create a compelling and SEO-friendly headline and subheadings for a blog post about [Topic], incorporating the main keywords.

4) Now that we have the headline and subheadings, provide an outline for a blog post about [Topic], with each section addressing one of the chosen common questions.

5) With the outline in place, for each section of the [Topic] blog post, provide supporting points or key messages that can be developed into informative and engaging content, along with relevant statistics, facts, or examples.

6) Let's discuss the best practices in on-page SEO for a blog post about [Topic], such as optimal keyword density, URL structure, meta descriptions, and image alt text.

7) Now, generate the introduction for the blog post about [Topic], incorporating the headline, main keywords, and a brief overview of the content.

8) Thanks! Generate the content for the first section (Subheading 1) of the [Topic] blog post, based on the supporting points, key messages, and SEO best practices.

Repeat step 8 for each subheading or section, modifying the subheading number accordingly.

9) Great work! Now, generate the conclusion for the blog post about [Topic], summarising the main points and providing a call-to-action for the readers.

10) Finally, for each section of the [Topic] blog post, provide an image prompt for a text-to-image AI tool in the following format: '[6-word description of the image or visual], [4 adjectives further describing the visual separated by commas], [the visual style (keep it consistent throughout)]'.

Here's an example of a 10-step chain prompt for writing a blog post with great SEO performance:

Let's walk through the first few steps of this 10 step chain prompt together, so we get a better understanding of how this works. For my example my topic will be dogs, so my first prompt will be:

"ChatGPT, please provide a list of common questions related to dogs."

 Sure! Here are some common questions related to dogs:

1. What breeds of dogs are good with kids?
2. How much exercise does a dog need per day?
3. How do I train my dog to stop barking excessively?
4. What is the best way to introduce a new dog to my current dog?
5. How often should I bathe my dog?
6. What are some common health issues that dogs face?
7. How can I tell if my dog is sick or in pain?
8. What are some good toys for dogs to play with?
9. How can I prevent my dog from chewing on furniture or shoes?
10. What should I do if my dog is aggressive towards other dogs or people?

I hope this helps! Let me know if you have any other questions.

I then follow up directly with the next prompt in the current chain:

Based on the provided list of questions, let's generate a list of popular keywords and phrases associated with dogs, focusing on high search volume and low competition."

 Sure, here's a list of popular keywords and phrases associated with dogs that have high search volume and low competition:

1. Dog breeds for families with kids
2. Dog exercise requirements
3. How to stop excessive barking in dogs
4. Introducing a new dog to current dog
5. Dog bathing frequency
6. Common dog health issues
7. Signs of sickness or pain in dogs
8. Best dog toys for playtime
9. Preventing dog chewing on furniture and shoes
10. Dealing with aggressive dogs

"From the list of common questions and keywords, please choose the most relevant ones and create a compelling and SEO-friendly headline and subheadings for a blog post about dogs, incorporating the main keywords."

 Sure, here's an example of a compelling and SEO-friendly headline and subheadings for a blog post about dogs:

Headline:

10 Things Every Dog Owner Should Know: From Exercise to Aggression

Subheadings:

1. Best Dog Breeds for Families with Kids: A Comprehensive Guide
2. Exercise is Key: How Much Exercise Does Your Dog Really Need?
3. Excessive Barking: How to Stop it Before It Becomes a Problem
4. Introducing a New Dog to Your Household: Tips and Tricks for Success
5. Bathing Your Dog: How Often Should You Do It?
6. Common Health Issues in Dogs: What You Need to Know
7. Signs of Sickness or Pain in Dogs: How to Recognize Them
8. Playtime for Pups: The Best Toys for Your Furry Friend
9. Preventing Destructive Chewing: Tips for a Safe and Happy Home
10. Dealing with Aggressive Dogs: How to Keep Your Pup and Others Safe

This headline and subheadings cover the main topics and keywords related to dogs that people might be interested in learning about. It's important to remember to write quality content that's informative, engaging, and helpful to readers while also incorporating the keywords to improve the article's search engine optimization (SEO).

Remember that ChatGPT has a context limit, which is the maximum amount of text it can take into account when creating a reply. For GPT-3.5, the context limit is around 1,400 words in English. If the chain prompt goes beyond this limit, ChatGPT might not remember all of the previous steps, which sometimes leads to ChatGPT filling in the blanks with what you could have asked for instead of what you actually asked for. Going beyond 10 steps may be more difficult for ChatGPT to stay coherent.

Thankfully, GPT-4, the latest version of the AI model, has a significantly larger context limit—4 times larger than GPT-3.5 for now, with another model in beta testing that's limit is 16 times larger than GPT-3.5's. This ability to handle extra context makes GPT-4 more suitable for Chain Prompting, as it can handle more extensive and complex prompts without losing track of the context. This allows you to create longer, more detailed chain prompts, helping ChatGPT produce even more precise and well-structured content, just like with our current example of writing SEO-optimised blog posts.

Exercise

Ready to give Chain Prompting a try? Grab the 10-step chain prompt we shared earlier for creating a blog post and replace the term [Topic] with any topic that interests you. ChatGPT will assist you in crafting a well-organised, SEO-friendly blog post in no time.

As you go through the chain prompts, be aware of the context limit. If ChatGPT struggles to recall previous steps, think about how you can remind it of the key elements needed for the next steps. You can do this by adding relevant keywords, context, or main points from prior steps in your prompts, making sure that the generated content remains consistent and focused.

By giving Chain Prompting a shot and adjusting the prompts to suit your needs, you'll gain a deeper understanding of how this technique can maximise ChatGPT's capabilities. Remember, practice is essential! The more you use Chain Prompting, the better you'll become at guiding the AI through intricate tasks and producing top-notch content tailored to your objectives.

You can find the 10 step chain prompt here to make copying and pasting easier: https://www.chatgpttrainings.com/chain-prompt

Use this space to write down your thoughts, tips & tricks!

14

THE RISE OF
AUTONOMOUS AGENTS

AI is always changing. After you've gotten the hang of prompt engineering with ChatGPT, you might be asking, "what's next?" The answer: autonomous agents. They're an advanced form of AI that brings new capabilities and functions, pushing beyond the limits of traditional AI models. Let's dive into this next stage of AI.

To get a handle on autonomous agents, let's define them. Simply put, an autonomous agent is an AI system that can work on its own to meet certain goals. It can make decisions, adjust to changes, and carry out tasks without needing a human to step in.

But how are autonomous agents different from familiar AI models like ChatGPT? While ChatGPT excels at processing prompts and producing related responses, it relies heavily on the prompts it's given. It's essentially reactive, reacting to the inputs provided to it.

In contrast, autonomous agents are proactive. They're not just waiting around for prompts; they're actively working within a task management system, learning and adapting to finish their designated tasks. They break down your original prompt into sub tasks, and then revaluate what they should do once their current task has been completed, essentially prompting itself to completion.

Here is a diagram created by Guodong (Troy) Zhao to help visualise what these autonomous agents are doing. While ChatGPT would move straight from 'set original objective' to 'give final answer', autonomous agents go through a longer process.

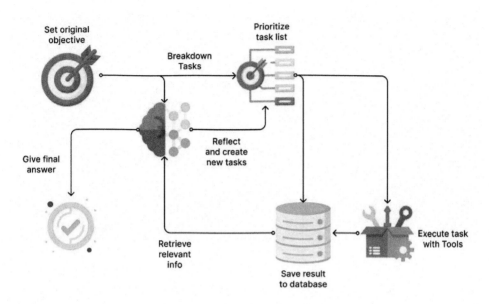

What's the benefit of all this? Autonomous agents can manage a broader set of tasks and can learn and get better based on the tasks they're given. They can also provide clear reporting, meaning they can relay their progress and results in a way that humans can comprehend. In summary, autonomous agents enhance AI functionality, offering adaptable and ongoing operation that moves AI towards truly independent action.

Now, let's put this into practice with GodMode.space, an online autonomous agent powered by ChatGPT. For this example, let's say I've given the agent the task: "I want to open a cat pyjama company in London, UK. Do a full market analysis."

When you head over to GodMode.space, you're greeted by a minimalistic interface. The central feature is a text box where you input your task. For our example, I've typed our cat pyjama market analysis task here, and then I clicked 'launch'.

With the click of the 'launch' button, the autonomous agent springs into action. It works through each task, revealing its thoughts, the reasoning behind those thoughts, and the steps it proposes to take next. If its suggestions align with my intentions, I can click 'approve'. If not, I can provide feedback to help guide its next actions.

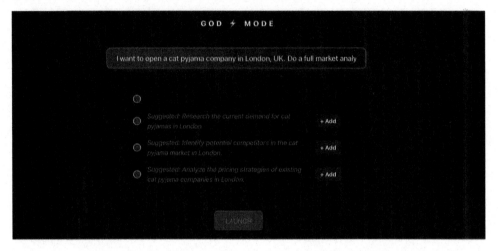

With the click of the 'launch' button, the autonomous agent springs into action. It works through each task, revealing its thoughts, the reasoning behind those thoughts, and the steps it proposes to take next. If its suggestions align with my intentions, I can click 'approve'. If not, I can provide feedback to help guide its next actions.

To save time, I also have the option to 'auto approve'. For the following 10 minutes, every proposed action will automatically get the green light, saving me from having to manually approve each step.

On the left-hand side of the interface, I can track the agent's progress with each subtask. Whenever it finds relevant information, it'll create a text document, jotting down these findings for me to review later. This allows me to see the market analysis taking shape in real-time.

By giving the AI a goal and letting it work, we're stepping into the future of AI technology: autonomous agents. They're not just reactive tools but proactive assistants, capable of navigating dynamic environments and tasks, learning and adapting as they go. From initial task to final results, this is the power and promise of autonomous agents in action.

Locally Installed Autonomous Agents

If you're a developer or someone who enjoys a DIY approach, installing your own autonomous agent might be right up your alley. This gives you a lot more control, and with a bit of tweaking, can deliver impressive results. Two notable options you can install yourself are BabyAGI and Auto-GPT, both available on GitHub.

BabyAGI is a great choice if you're looking for something simple to start with. It's like a basic model of an autonomous agent, and it's user-friendly enough for beginners. The real strength of BabyAGI is its flexibility. You can build on its basic framework, adapting it for different tasks, from sorting your emails to helping with coding. Plus, it's compatible with a variety of OpenAI models, as well as the Llama model, so you've got plenty of scope for experimenting.

```
OBJECTIVE = "Write a weather report for SF today"

llm = OpenAI(temperature=0)

# Logging of LLMChains
verbose=False
# If None, will keep on going forever
max_iterations: Optional[int] = 3
baby_agi = BabyAGI.from_llm(
    llm=llm,
    vectorstore=vectorstore,
    verbose=verbose,
    max_iterations=max_iterations
)

baby_agi({"objective": OBJECTIVE})
```

On the other hand, Auto-GPT is a powerhouse when it comes to handling data from multiple sources. This makes it stand out from typical AI models. It can pull in information from news articles, scientific databases, and even integrate with Google Search, Google Places, and Wikipedia. This makes Auto-GPT perfect for tasks that need real-time data and diverse sources.

So, if you're up for a bit of setup work, these autonomous agents can be installed on your own computer to run tasks for you. Check them out on GitHub, grab your OpenAI API key, and you'll be ready to dive into the world of self-installed autonomous agents.

Use this space to write down your thoughts, tips & tricks!

15

USING CHATGPT WITHOUT USING CHATGPT

If you want to harness the power of ChatGPT but the servers are at capacity, don't worry! There is another option. ChatGPT, also known as GPT-3.5, is a user-friendly platform that takes OpenAI's latest iteration of their GPT models and trains it to become a safe chatbot accessible to the general public. However, you can also access the model directly through OpenAI's Playground.

Head over to https://platform.openai.com/playground to log in with your ChatGPT credentials. The page may appear complex at first, but it's primarily meant for developers. Don't be intimidated, we'll break down each aspect and show you how it works.

Note: This playground is technically a paid-for space, however the costs work out about $0.02 / 700 words used, and you start with $18 credit for your first 3 months.

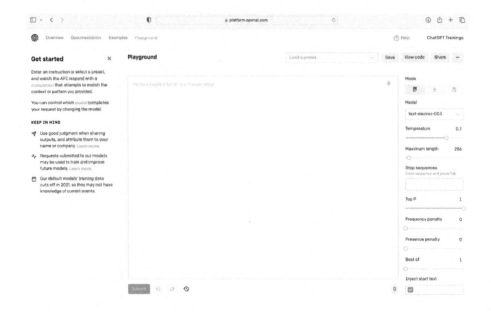

Instead of a chatbot, think of the Playground as an autocompletion tool. It's like writing in your diary and answering your own questions. To test it out, I wrote *'I've had a lot on my mind recently. Maybe I should use this weekend to give myself space. Mmmmm... What activities could I do?'* in the text field and hit submit. The Playground generated several suggestions for activities I could do to find headspace. You can continue the conversation by clicking at the bottom of the text and typing more.

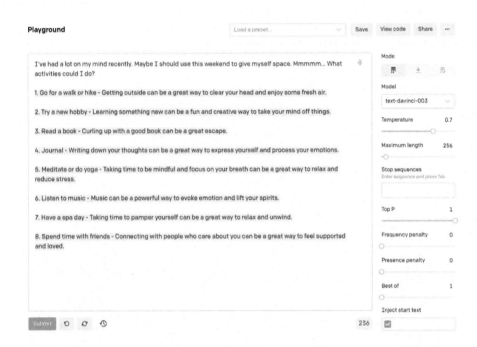

On the top and right side of the text field, you'll see a list of parameters that allow you to customise your AI assistant. Let's take a look at a few essential ones together.

Load a Preset

On the top of the page, you'll see a dropdown menu labeled 'Load a preset...'. This is where you can access a list of pre-made examples. These examples can show you the best practices suggested by OpenAI when creating prompts in the playground. Keep in mind that what works well here may not work the same in ChatGPT and vice versa.

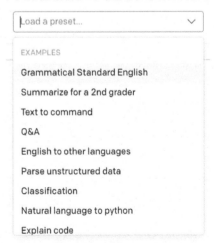

Models

Models in the context of GPT-3 are like recipes for a computer program to follow to complete a task. Different models have different instructions and ways of doing things, so selecting the right model can help you get the results you want.

When choosing a model, you consider the task you want to complete and the type of results you're looking for. For example, if you want a fast response and real-time interaction, you might choose a model that has been optimised for speed. If you're looking for high accuracy, you might choose a larger model that has been trained on more data.

Davinci-003   Curie-001   Babbage-001   Ada-001

For most users, sticking with the Davinci-003 model is probably the best choice. This model is the most powerful and provides the best performance in terms of accuracy and speed. It is ideal for those who want the best results and don't have to worry too much about cost.

However, for developers who need to consider the trade-off between speed, quality, and cost, the other models may be more suitable. For example, if you're working on a smaller project or need a fast response, you might choose a model like Ada-001 that has been optimised for speed. Or if you're on a tight budget, you might choose a model like Babbage-001 that offers basic functionality at a low cost.

Maximum Length

The maximum length parameter sets the limit for how much the AI should write, measured in units of tokens. It controls the amount of text that the model generates.

A token in Natural Language Processing (NLP) is a unit of meaning, which can be a single character, syllable, or word. In English, 1 token is roughly equivalent to 0.7 words. In other languages, the number of tokens per word can be much higher.

To give you an idea, if you set the maximum length parameter to 200, the AI will generate a response that is no longer than around 140 words in English.

This parameter can be useful if you want to make sure the AI doesn't generate too much text. For instance, you might want the AI to write a short answer to a question, or a caption for a picture. In these cases, you might set the maximum length parameter to 50 or 100.

On the other hand, if you want the AI to generate a longer response, like a story or an article, you might set the Max Tokens parameter to a higher number, such as 500 or 1000.

In this example, I limited the maximum number of tokens to 100. Since I asked for an essay, GPT-3 was ready to write more but had to stop in the middle of a sentence because it reached the 100 token limit.

For the davinci-003 model, you can set the limit up to 4000 tokens. This includes both the text you enter and the response from GPT-3. In simple terms, the total number of tokens in the text box and your maximum limit should not be more than 4000.

Temperature

The temperature parameter in GPT-3 determines the amount of "surprise" or randomness in the output generated by the model. The higher the temperature, the more likely the model is to generate unexpected or diverse responses, while the lower the temperature, the more conservative or predictable the response will be.

Temperature   1

For example, if you set the temperature to 1.0, the model is likely to generate responses that are more creative, diverse, and unpredictable. On the other hand, if you set the temperature to 0.5, the model is more likely to generate responses that are more accurate, conservative, and predictable.

For most users, a temperature value between 0.5 and 1.0 is a good starting point. This gives the model enough room to generate interesting and diverse responses, while still maintaining a good level of accuracy and predictability. However, the optimal temperature value will depend on the specific needs and requirements of your use case.

So, the temperature parameter gives you control over the amount of randomness or unpredictability in the model's output, and you can adjust it as needed to achieve the best results for your specific needs.

Frequency Penalty

The frequency penalty parameter can be especially useful in preventing the model from generating repetitive outputs that can be funny, but also annoying.

For example, let's say you're chatting with GPT-3 and you asked it a question. If the frequency penalty is set to a low value, GPT-3 might start every response with the same phrase, like "Well, my friend, the answer is...". While it might be funny at first, it could quickly become repetitive and annoying.

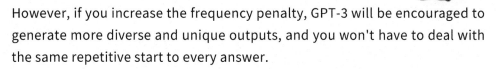

However, if you increase the frequency penalty, GPT-3 will be encouraged to generate more diverse and unique outputs, and you won't have to deal with the same repetitive start to every answer.

So, the frequency penalty allows you to control the diversity of the model's output, preventing it from generating repetitive responses. You can adjust it to find the right balance between diverse and predictable responses, so that you can have a fun and engaging conversation with GPT-3.

Presence Penalty

The presence penalty parameter affects how much the model prioritises including specific words or phrases in its output.

For example, let's say you're using GPT-3 to write a story and you want the main character's name to appear in every sentence. If you set the presence penalty to a high value, GPT-3 will be more likely to include the character's name in every sentence, even if it makes the sentence sound awkward.

On the other hand, if you set the presence penalty to a low value, GPT-3 will be more likely to generate sentences that flow well and are grammatically correct, but the character's name might not appear as often as you'd like.

So, the presence penalty allows you to control how much the model prioritises including specific words or phrases in its output. You can adjust it to find the right balance between including the words you want and generating grammatically correct and fluent sentences.

Now you have everything you need to be able to use the power of ChatGPT even when the AI tool has reached maximum capacity.

Use this space to write down your thoughts, tips & tricks!

PART IV
GPT-4

AI IS MOVING AT SUCH A FAST PACE THAT WE CAN HARDLY
PREDICT WHERE IT WILL BE IN A FEW YEARS,
BUT WE KNOW IT'S GOING TO BE EXTRAORDINARY.

FEI-FEI LI

1 6

GETTING ACCESS TO GPT-4

If you're eager to explore the capabilities of GPT-4, you're in luck! GPT-4 is currently available for ChatGPT Plus subscribers, and OpenAI is considering making it accessible to free users in the near future.

ChatGPT Plus is a subscription plan that costs $20 per month. Subscribers are able to use GPT-4 and can take advantage of some of the new features that we cover in this section. However, it's important to note that there is a current limit of 100 messages per 4 hours for GPT-4 usage.

Now, let's dive into the step-by-step process of upgrading to ChatGPT Plus and switching to the GPT-4 model.

Step 1: Find the option to upgrade.
To begin, you'll need to locate the option to upgrade to ChatGPT Plus. This can be found on the bottom left-hand side of the page, where you'll see an "Upgrade" button.

Step 2: Review the pricing details and comparison.

Once you've clicked on the upgrade option, a box will appear displaying the pricing details and a comparison between the free and Plus plans. This is your opportunity to review the differences between the two plans and ensure that ChatGPT Plus aligns with your needs.

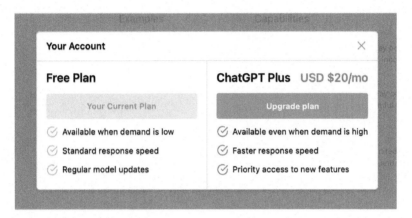

Step 3: Upgrade to ChatGPT Plus

If you're satisfied with the details and ready to upgrade, follow the on-screen prompts to complete the subscription process. You'll be required to provide payment information to set this up.

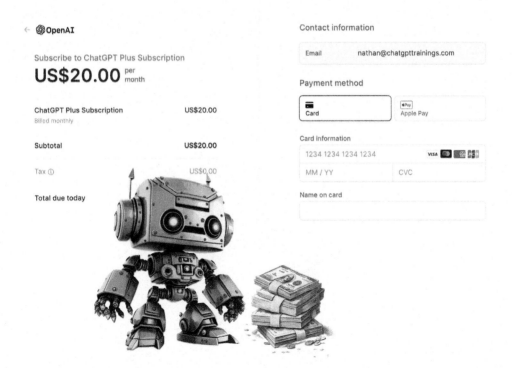

Step 4: Change from the GPT-3.5 model to the GPT-4 Model

To use GPT-4, you need to open a new chat. By default, the chat will be set to GPT-3.5. However, at the top of the chat window, you'll find a dropdown menu where you can change the current model to GPT-4

Model
GPT-4

Default (GPT-3.5)

GPT-4

Our most advanced model, available to Plus subscribers.

Legacy (GPT-3.5)

GPT-4 excels at tasks that require advanced reasoning, complex instruction understanding, and more creativity.

GPT-4 ✓

Reasoning

Speed

Conciseness

ChatGPT PLUS

Accessing GPT-4 through ChatGPT Plus is a straightforward process, although you won't currently have access to system messages and image input yet (see the next chapters for more information). While my aim isn't to promote ChatGPT Plus, I wanted to put together a simple walkthrough for those who want early access to GPT-4's advanced features. By following these steps, you'll be able to harness the power of GPT-4 and explore its potential to revolutionise your work, projects, or AI experimentation.

17

THE HYPE WAS WRONG

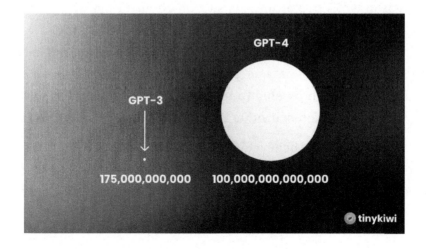

In the era of social media, separating facts from fiction has become increasingly important, especially in the rapidly evolving world of AI advancements. This chapter focuses on a notable case of AI misinformation: the hype surrounding GPT-4 and the consequences of spreading false information about its capabilities.

The seed of misinformation about GPT-4's capabilities was planted back in 2021 when a Wired article quoted a conversation between Andrew Feldman, CEO of AI hardware startup Cerebras Systems, and OpenAI. Feldman claimed that GPT-4 would have 100 trillion parameters, a statement that OpenAI later denied at the end of 2022. Despite the denial, the false claim spread quickly on social media platforms like Twitter, LinkedIn, and Reddit, leading to inflated expectations and hype surrounding GPT-4.

This infographic started to spread across social media at the beginning of 2023, it claimed that GPT-4 would have 100 trillion parameters and will make GPT-3 look tiny in comparison.

The hype-train had set off and was not prepared to slow down. Another infographic surfaced the day before GPT-4 launched, claiming that the new model would supporting text, images, videos, and audio inputs, making it multimodal. Even after OpenAI officially released GPT-4 and stated that it supported text and image, people continued to share the infographic, boasting about GPT-4's new features.

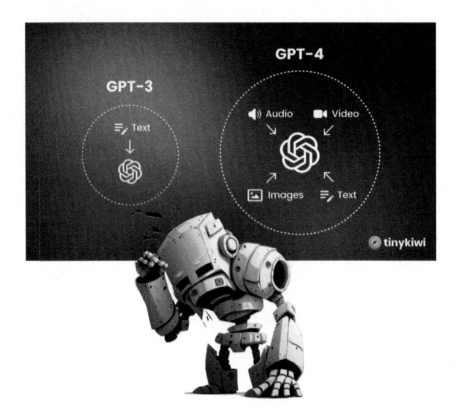

The reason why I'm starting this section about GPT-4 with this cautionary tale is because I don't want you to feel disappointed by the reality of what OpenAI released. GPT-4 doesn't process audio or video, nor does it have 1,000 times as many parameters as its predecessor. If, like me, you are fortunate enough to be able to test out GPT-4 straight away, you may not even notice any difference, other than a logo change and a slower output.

This being said, I do believe GPT-4 is a game-changer. Over the next few chapters we'll explore some of the recent upgrades that are either already live or are coming soon, and understand why OpenAI's new model is truly revolutionary.

18

MORE CONTEXT = MORE POWER

My favorite upgrade is the dramatic increase in the size of the context ChatGPT can handle, from 2,000 tokens in GPT-3.5 to a staggering 32,000 tokens in GPT-4. This remarkable leap allows for a greater understanding of complex texts and the potential to revolutionize how we approach problem-solving, communication, and more.

Before we dive too deep into this topic, let's understand what tokens are and why they are so essential in language models. In the context of AI and natural language processing, a token represents a unit of text, such as a word or a character, that the model processes. As humans, we divide our language up into sentences, words, syllables, and characters; these language models do something quite similar. The more tokens a language model can handle, the more context it can take into account, leading to better comprehension and more accurate responses. In simple terms, a larger number of tokens means the AI model can consider more information when processing and generating text, which dramatically improves its performance.

magine that you have a 20-page document, and you want ChatGPT to ensure that the writing style is coherent, that paragraphs flow into one another, and that there are no grammar or spelling mistakes. With GPT-4, this could all be done in a single prompt.

Another example where I can see myself using GPT-4's increased context capacity is to summarize lengthy documents, such as research papers, training handouts, or reports. GPT-3.5's token limitation meant that it could only process a fraction of the text, potentially missing crucial information. We could circumnavigate this by dividing the text up, giving it to ChatGPT piece by piece, asking for summaries one at a time, copying and pasting the summaries into another document, and then asking ChatGPT to summarize the summaries. In contrast, GPT-4 can do this in a single prompt.

Imagine you wanted to set up an in-depth simulation that requires an extensive understanding of previous interactions. GPT-3.5 would struggle to recall earlier parts of the conversation, leading to inconsistencies and irrelevant responses. However, thanks to GPT-4's increased token capacity, ChatGPT can now provide more consistent, context-aware, and relevant responses, as it has a broader understanding of the whole conversation.

As you can see, the dramatic increase in the amount of context ChatGPT can use thanks to GPT-4's new features can have a huge impact on the AI's performance and potential applications. With this new superpower, we can now try out more complex, nuanced, and intricate problems, and continue to push the boundaries of what AI can achieve.

MULTIMODAL: IMAGE INPUT

The most talked about new feature of GPT-4 is its ability to work with image inputs. This opens up new opportunities for communication, collaboration, and creativity. Unlike DALL.E or MidJourney, GPT-4 doesn't output images, instead it can take them in as an input, break them down into human language, and then use that language as context for your prompt.

Imagine being able to draw a mock up of a website on a piece of paper, take a picture of it, and ask ChatGPT to write the code to bring your idea to life. Greg Brockman, President and Co-Founder of OpenAI, did exactly that during his developer live-stream of GPT-4.

Since GPT-4 is able to understand both image and text inputs, plus bring them together, this new model could have very creative use cases that go beyond ChatGPT's current capabilities such as:

Design Feedback: AI models can analyse design mockups or wireframes and provide constructive feedback or suggestions for improvement.

Creative Collaboration: Artists and designers can use AI-generated text based on visual inputs to brainstorm ideas, create narratives, or explore new artistic concepts.

Visual Storytelling: AI models can interpret a series of images, generating captivating and coherent stories or descriptions.

Educational Support: AI can help students by analysing complex diagrams or visual aids, providing detailed explanations or simplifying intricate concepts.

Let's take a concrete example OpenAI provided in their documentation about GPT-4 to see how this could look like:

User: What is funny about this image?
Describe it panel by panel.

GPT-4:   The image shows a package for a "Lightning Cable" adapter with three panels.

Panel 1: A smartphone with a VGA connector (a large, blue, 15-pin connector typically used for computer monitors) plugged into its charging port.

Panel 2: The package for the "Lightning Cable" adapter with a picture of a VGA connector on it.

Panel 3: A close-up of the VGA connector with a small Lightning connector (used for charging iPhones and other Apple devices) at the end.

The humor in this image comes from the absurdity of plugging a large, outdated VGA connector into a small, modern smartphone charging port.

While this feature is still in its research phase and not publicly available, the possibilities it offers are truly exciting.

MORE ACCURATE
BUT STILL PROBABILISTIC

Each new iteration of OpenAI's GPT models has been getting better and better at providing factual information and answering questions correctly, with GPT-4 pushing the envelope even further. However, even this model isn't perfect, which means that GPT-4 still sometimes makes up facts and sources that are simply not true.

GPT-4, like its predecessors, is a probabilistic machine. Its main job is to predict the most likely next word in a given context. When trying to give factual information, GPT-4 doesn't do research to find the right answer; instead, it comes up with responses based on patterns and associations it picked up during its training. As a result, the model's outputs are usually spot-on or super convincing, and that's the problem; ChatGPT is very sure of its output even when it's "hallucinating." Thankfully, GPT-4 seems to be better at staying away from made-up information than its predecessors.

Here's an example of how GPT-3.5 makes up sources:

 Give me the URLs of 3 articles from 2020 about climate change

 Sure, here are three articles from 2020 about climate change:

1. "Climate Change Is Making Hurricane Season Worse — and More Dangerous" - published on September 11, 2020, by Time Magazine. URL: **https://time.com/5887366/hurricane-season-climate-change/**

2. "Climate change: Summers could become 'too hot for humans'" - published on August 4, 2020, by BBC News. URL: **https://www.bbc.com/news/science-environment-53698069**

3. "2020 Tied for Warmest Year on Record, NASA Analysis Shows" - published on January 14, 2021, by NASA. URL: **https://www.nasa.gov/press-release/2020-tied-for-warmest-year-on-record-nasa-analysis-shows**

The first two URLs are made up and don't work, but ChatGPT seemed very confident that they would. Let's take the first URL from the Times to understand how this happened: https://time.com/5887366/hurricane-season-climate-change/. ChatGPT has seen many URLs with this kind of format in its training data, so it must have learned a certain pattern:

[https://time.com/][7-digit number][article title with hyphens]

Since ChatGPT is a probabilistic machine, it looked at the context of my prompt, thought about the URLs it had seen in the past, and built this one for me.

GPT-4, however, didn't fall for this trick.

Give me the URLs of 3 articles from 2020 about climate change

 As an AI language model, I cannot browse the internet or provide real-time data. However, I can recommend some articles from 2020 that discuss climate change. You can search for these articles using their titles and publication names. Here are three well-known articles:

1. Title: "A Very Bad Year for Earth's Climate"
   Publication: The New York Times
   Author: Henry Fountain
   Date: October 14, 2020
2. Title: "The World's Climate Catastrophe Worsens Amid Pandemic"
   Publication: The Guardian
   Author: Fiona Harvey
   Date: August 21, 2020
3. Title: "How the Pandemic Is Affecting CO2 Emissions"
   Publication: Scientific American
   Author: Chelsea Harvey
   Date: April 28, 2020

To access these articles, simply search for their titles in your preferred search engine, and you should be able to find the relevant URLs.

GPT-4 was more aware of the fact that it wouldn't be able to output the URLs with a high level of accuracy, so instead it decided to share the titles of the articles and asked me to use a search engine to find the URLs. Accuracy isn't just about getting things right, but also about being more cautious when its output could be wrong.

This new accuracy upgrade has led to GPT-4 having human-level performance on various professional and academic benchmarks, like scoring in the top 10% on a simulated bar exam. Below is a chart from OpenAI that shows how GPT-4 did compared to GPT-3.5 on various exams.

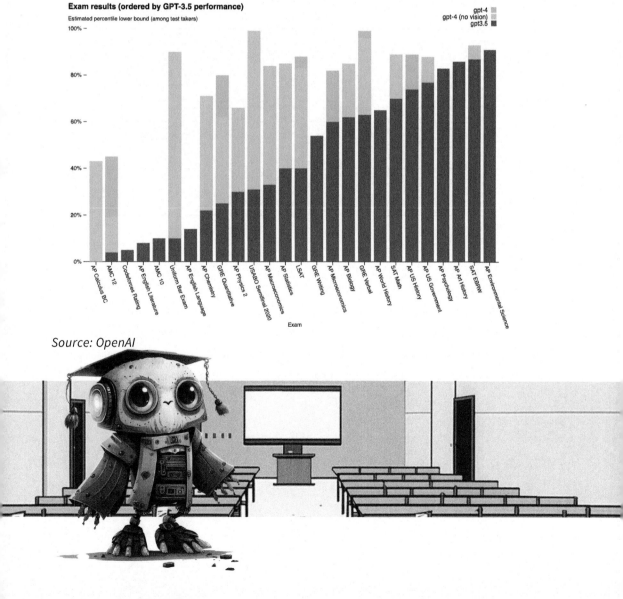

Source: OpenAI

Another cool thing about GPT-4 is how well it performs in multiple languages. The model beats GPT-3.5 and other LLMs in 24 out of 26 languages tested, even in low-resource languages like Latvian, Welsh, and Swahili. This is great to hear, as AI models shouldn't just revolutionise the English-speaking world, but the entire multilingual globe.

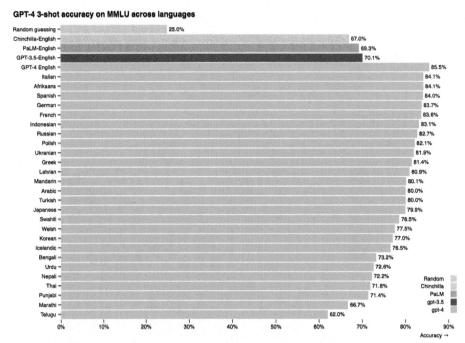

Source: OpenAI

Higher accuracy is the main upgrade you'll be able to quickly notice between GPT-3.5 and GPT-4 until OpenAI releases the system message and image input features. Personally, I feel way more confident using ChatGPT for research purposes now that GPT-4 is available, and I think this could open up many more use cases in the education sector and in the workplace.

CHATGPT WITH WEB BROWSING

In previous chapters, we've discussed the incredible abilities of ChatGPT. However, it had a limitation. The knowledge of ChatGPT was capped at 2021. So, if you asked a question about something that happened after that date, it would remind you of this fact. But now, a significant development has changed that.

Now, ChatGPT can access the internet, sort of. It's not like you and me browsing the web, but it's a big step forward. The way it works might surprise you. And setting it up is a straightforward process.

Here's how you can set up internet browsing for ChatGPT:

1 **Upgrade to ChatGPT Plus:** As of the time of writing this chapter, in June 2023, the feature of internet browsing is only available with ChatGPT Plus.

2 **Go to Settings:** This is where you can adjust how OpenAI uses your data, and where you can activate Beta features.

3 **Enable Internet Browsing in the Beta Features:** By doing this, you will have the option for ChatGPT to use the web when it thinks it's necessary.

4 **Switch to GPT-4 and Select Internet Browsing:** This final step completes the process and opens up a new dimension of possibilities with ChatGPT.

Here is a screenshot to show you how this new interface looks like, how activate the beta features, and then how to use this version of GPT-4.

Now, with these steps completed, ChatGPT has the potential to pull in the most recent information available online. It's a new age in AI capability. But remember, it's not quite like traditional internet browsing. It's more like ChatGPT has a reading assistant who can quickly look things up for it. It's an exciting development that pushes the boundaries of what we can achieve with ChatGPT.

How Does Web Browsing Work?

To learn how to get the most out of this new feature, we need to start by understanding how internet browsing works with ChatGPT. Remember, ChatGPT is a language model that predicts the next word in a sentence based on the context provided. The concept of internet browsing adds a new dimension to this. It passes more recent and relevant information to ChatGPT, along with your prompt, which is different from how ChatGPT uses its pre-training dataset.

ChatGPT's pre-training dataset and internet access are two different aspects of its operation. To make this clearer, let's consider an example. If you ask ChatGPT to describe how people feel about the Star Wars Prequel, it doesn't refer back to specific information about the films or people's reactions. Rather, during its training, it read a vast number of articles, books, blog posts, and online discussions about this topic and similar ones. In doing so, it learned the common words and themes associated with these discussions.

Because of this extensive reading, ChatGPT can respond with a great deal of insight, based on the patterns it observed in the many sources it was trained on. It doesn't recall specific articles or discussions, but it uses the patterns it learned to generate responses that match the context.

To understand the difference that internet browsing brings, let's walk through what ChatGPT does when it uses this feature.

1 **Deciding if browsing is needed:** ChatGPT first assesses whether it needs to use the internet to respond to your question. Not every interaction needs internet browsing.

2 **Creating a search prompt:** If internet browsing is needed, ChatGPT creates a search prompt using relevant keywords, rather than conversational language, and starts a search using Bing.

3 **Reading web content:** Think of ChatGPT as a personal assistant using a computer. It clicks on one of the search results and starts to read the content.

4 **Searching for more information:** ChatGPT continues to browse, hopping between websites and sometimes conducting new searches, until it feels it has gathered enough information.

(5) **Adding context to your prompt:** The browser tool takes the newly-found web content and sends it to ChatGPT as context to pair with your original prompt.

(6) **Providing a response:** Finally, ChatGPT returns a response to your original prompt, but now with the additional context supplied by the web browsing feature.

This new process is different to how ChatGPT uses its original pre-training dataset. Previously, ChatGPT's responses were influenced by many different sources. However, when browsing the web, ChatGPT captures information from just a few sources. The main difference here is that the perspective ChatGPT provides is based on the limited number of new information sources it found.

For example, if you're deciding whether to watch a new film and want a summary of critic opinions, ChatGPT's output will be based on the perspectives of the websites it selected. While the browsing feature allows ChatGPT to access fresh information, this information represents a narrow range of perspectives and carries the biases of the few sources it retrieved.

This addition of web browsing capabilities is an incredible step forward for ChatGPT. It opens up a wealth of new possibilities and makes ChatGPT more revolutionary than ever before. However, keep in mind that it doesn't mean ChatGPT has complete access to the internet with every prompt. Web browsing is a tool to pull in current information when needed, but it doesn't replace the broad base of knowledge ChatGPT has from its pre-training. We will still need to discover best practices and prompt engineering techniques to make web browsing with ChatGPT more efficient and reliable. So expect another update to this book soon.

2 2

CHATGPT PLUGINS

PlugIns are like the eyes and ears of ChatGPT, allowing it to see and interact with the world beyond its original training dataset. Think of them them as sets of instructions that ChatGPT has learned to use to connect to third-party services. These services could be anything from weather updates to flight booking systems.

It works in a similar way to ChatGPT's web browsing capability, which we covered in the previous chapter. Just as ChatGPT can use Bing to browse the web and find information, plugins pull new information from other sources. This new information is then added to your original prompt, providing ChatGPT with a richer context to generate its output.

Plugins revolutionise the way we can use ChatGPT. They open up a world of possibilities, transforming ChatGPT from a text generator into an incredible digital assistant. For example, if you're planning a trip, you could ask ChatGPT to find the best flight deals, the weather forecast for your destination, clothes that would be appropriate based on the weather, and even help you find and order them to your door. With the right set of plugin, ChatGPT's capabilities can reach far beyond anything we have seen so far.

Here are a few examples of plugins that are available today, however there are hundreds more, and new additions released on a regular cadence.

ScholarAI
Uninstall ⊗

Unlock the power of scientific research with peer-reviewed papers from PubMed, Arxiv, Springer, and more.

Show Me
Uninstall ⊗

Create and edit diagrams directly in chat.

Expedia
Uninstall ⊗

Bring your trip plans to life – get there, stay there, find things to see and do.

KAYAK
Uninstall ⊗

Search flights, stays & rental cars or get recommendations where you can go on your budget.

Video Insights
Install ↻

Interact with online video platforms like Youtube or Daily Motion.

Wolfram
Install ↻

Access computation, math, curated knowledge & real-time data through Wolfram|Alpha and Wolfram Language.

VoxScript
Uninstall ⊗

Enables searching of YouTube transcripts, financial data sources, and Google Search results, and more!

KeyMate.AI Search
Install ↻

Search&Browse the web by using Google Search results with KeyMate.AI, your AI-powered web crawler.

Prompt Perfect
Install ↻

Type 'perfect' to craft the perfect prompt, every time.

Speak
Install ↻

Learn how to say anything in another language with Speak, your AI-powered language tutor.

Zapier
Uninstall ⊗

Interact with over 5,000+ apps like Google Sheets, Gmail, HubSpot, Salesforce, and thousands more.

Link Reader
Uninstall ⊗

Reads the content of all kinds of links, like webpage, PDF, PPT, image, Word & other docs.

Bramework
Install ↻

Find keywords, generate content briefs, perform SEO analysis, and extract SEO information.

Open Trivia
Install ↻

Get trivia questions from various categories and difficulty levels.

Xweather
Install ↻

XWeather gives weather information for a location. Ask for the current weather, a 5-day forecast, or a radar image.

SceneXplain
Install ↻

SceneXplain lets you attach images to your prompt. Explore image storytelling beyond pixels.

Calorie Chat
Install ↻

Tracking what you eat doesn't have to be hard. With Calorie Chat, you'll find calorie counting simpler than ever...

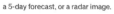
One Word Domains
Install ↻

Check the availability of a domain and compare prices across different registrars.

Let's dive into an example together. Imagine that we want to use ChatGPT to create an AI newsletter that brought together the latest developments in the AI world. We would normally start by doing some research, pulling some notes together, categorising the findings, and then writing it up as a newsletter. Here is an example of doing all of this using VoxScript plugin with ChatGPT: https://bit.ly/ai-newsletter-chatgpt

Make sure you read through this conversation before you move on to the next part.

Initially, we needed to find recent AI news. We asked ChatGPT to find YouTube videos covering the latest in AI. This is where the VoxScript plugin came into play. ChatGPT converted our prompt into a YouTube search, which VoxScript carried out, providing us with a list of relevant videos.

The next step was to extract the key information from these videos. We asked VoxScript to read the transcripts and list all the AI updates. This shows how plugins can extend ChatGPT's capabilities, allowing it to access and process information beyond its training data.

With the information from the transcripts, we started to craft our AI Newsletter. Using ChatGPT's conversational approach and the [format] technique, we structured the information into an easy-to-read format. We could build this is a chain-prompt and run it each week to create a new AI newsletter.

This is the power of plugins. They enable us to go beyond simple text generation to take advantage of third party systems to work with real-time data. They expand ChatGPT's capabilities, creating a world of new use cases.

PART V
USE CASES

I HEAR AND I FORGET.
I SEE AND I REMEMBER.
I DO AND I UNDERSTAND.

CONFUCIUS

If you are looking for lots of prompt examples and use cases you can head over to beta.openai.com/examples to help spark your creativity.

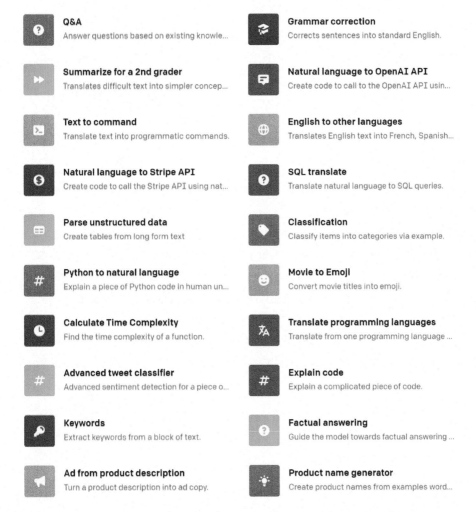

Q&A — Answer questions based on existing knowle...	**Grammar correction** — Corrects sentences into standard English.
Summarize for a 2nd grader — Translates difficult text into simpler concep...	**Natural language to OpenAI API** — Create code to call to the OpenAI API usin...
Text to command — Translate text into programmatic commands.	**English to other languages** — Translates English text into French, Spanish...
Natural language to Stripe API — Create code to call the Stripe API using nat...	**SQL translate** — Translate natural language to SQL queries.
Parse unstructured data — Create tables from long form text	**Classification** — Classify items into categories via example.
Python to natural language — Explain a piece of Python code in human un...	**Movie to Emoji** — Convert movie titles into emoji.
Calculate Time Complexity — Find the time complexity of a function.	**Translate programming languages** — Translate from one programming language ...
Advanced tweet classifier — Advanced sentiment detection for a piece o...	**Explain code** — Explain a complicated piece of code.
Keywords — Extract keywords from a block of text.	**Factual answering** — Guide the model towards factual answering ...
Ad from product description — Turn a product description into ad copy.	**Product name generator** — Create product names from examples word...

Over the past couple of months, I've seen post after post on social media and in the news about ways ChatGPT can improve productivity in the workplace. I love a great use case, but when I tried it out for myself, I realised it was more difficult than I first thought. What was lacking was some guidelines on how to best engineer my prompts to get the most out of the particular use case. So throughout these chapters, my focus will be less on the quantity of examples, as the webiste above can give you, and more on the quality of our exploration into them. This way, I hope you will learn how to use ChatGPT for these use cases more effectively.

After reading about each use case, open up ChatGPT and try it out for yourself. I always recommend learning by doing with ChatGPT.

23

BRAINSTOMRING IDEAS

ChatGPT can be a great way to come up with new ideas at work. By asking it to give you ideas about a specific topic, you can use it for your own personal brainstorming sessions. The great thing about ChatGPT is that it has access to a lot of information that is not easily accessible to humans. It has read more books, articles, and documents than any human could read in their lifetime. This makes it perfect assistant to help you come up with fresh and creative ideas. With its ability to understand and process a lot of information quickly, ChatGPT can help you think outside the box and generate new and innovative ideas that can help you or your business grow.

List 5 ideas ideas for a new approach to sustainable tourism that involves llamas.

1. Llama trekking: Offer guided llama treks through natural areas, allowing tourists to explore the wilderness while minimizing their impact on the environment.
2. Llama packing: Use llamas to transport supplies and equipment for camping or backpacking trips, reducing the need for motorized vehicles.
3. Llama farm tours: Offer tours of llama farms to educate visitors about sustainable agriculture and animal husbandry practices.
4. Llama therapy: Use llamas as therapy animals for stress relief and emotional well-being for visitors.
5. Llama volunteer work: Allow visitors to participate in llama conservation projects, such as habitat restoration and reintroduction efforts, to promote environmental stewardship.

One way we can brainstorming in a better way with ChatGPT is by creating a structure for the output. In real life, I often use a spreadsheet to organise my ideas. I write down different ideas in one column and add more details about each idea in other columns. This helps me understand each idea more fully. We can do the same with ChatGPT, by organising the ideas it generates in a structured format. This could include using columns for different aspects of the idea, such as potential benefits, drawbacks, and next steps. By doing this, we can gain a deeper understanding of each idea, its potential and its feasibility. This can help us make more informed decisions and take action on the best ideas. Let's give it a try with ChatGPT.

Let's brainstorm some ideas for a new approach to sustainable tourism that involves llamas. Write these in a table with the following format: idea name, short description, how is this sustainable, target market.

Idea Name	Short Description	How is this Sustainable	Target Market
Llama Trekking	Offering guided llama trekking tours through wilderness areas.	Llamas are low-impact animals and can carry supplies, reducing the need for motorized vehicles. Tour groups are small and focus on educating participants about conservation and sustainable practices.	Outdoor enthusiasts, hikers, and nature lovers.
Llama Pack Trips	Offering multi-day camping trips with llamas carrying all gear and supplies.	Llamas are low-impact animals and can carry supplies, reducing the need for motorized vehicles. Campsites are chosen for their minimal impact on the environment and education is provided on Leave No Trace principles.	Outdoor enthusiasts, hikers, and nature lovers.
Llama Yoga Retreats	Offering yoga retreats in beautiful wilderness areas with llamas present.	Llamas are low-impact animals and can be used to carry supplies, reducing the need for motorized vehicles. Retreats focus on mindfulness, self-care, and connection with nature.	Yoga enthusiasts and people looking for a unique and sustainable way to relax and rejuvenate.

Another way to improve brainstorming with ChatGPT is by using it to help jumpstart your creativity. One technique I like to use is to come up with bad ideas that won't work. These "bad" ideas can sometimes be the spark we need to think of a new and innovative idea that was just out of reach with our usual way of thinking. Using ChatGPT to generate a variety of ideas, including some that might seem bad or unworkable, can help us to think more creatively and come up with truly unique and innovative solutions.

> Let's brainstorm some ideas for a new approach to sustainable tourism that involves llamas. List 5 ideas of bsuiness ideas that won't work. Prioritise crazy and bizzar ideas.

1. Llama-powered hot air balloon rides: While it may seem like a unique and exciting idea, it is likely not practical or safe to harness llamas to power a hot air balloon.
2. Llama-drawn carriage tours through busy city streets: Not only would this put the llamas at risk of injury, it would also be disruptive to traffic and potentially dangerous for pedestrians.
3. Llama-assisted rock climbing excursions: Llamas are not built for climbing and would not be able to assist in this type of activity.
4. Llama-led safari adventures: Llamas are not native to safari habitats and would not be able to navigate or survive in those environments.
5. Llama-staffed luxury hotel: Llamas are not trained for customer service, and would not be able to provide the level of comfort and amenities that guests expect from a luxury hotel.

You can combine the tools and techniques we covered in this book with these brainstorming methods to get more creative outputs.

- Give feedback to ChatGPT
- Roleplay as a creative person/character you like
- Train it on examples of ideas you like
- Explore each idea thoroughly, one at a time.

24

TRANSLATION

ChatGPT has been trained on many different languages, making it a powerful machine learning (ML) translation tool... if you know how to use it correctly. Before we start, it's important to keep in mind that the quality of translations in a particular language depends on the amount of content in that language that was used to train ChatGPT.

From my experience, the results for French and Spanish were much better than those for Macedonian. With that said, let's dive in and see how we can use ChatGPT for translations in the best way possible.

Translate this poem, keeping the same format

translate this into english:

私と小鳥と鈴と

私が両手をひろげても、
お空はちっとも飛べないが、
飛べる小鳥は私のやうに、
地面(じべた)を速くは走れない。

私がからだをゆすっても、
きれいな音は出ないけど、
あの鳴る鈴は私のやうに、
たくさんな唄は知らないよ。

鈴と、小鳥と、それから私、
みんなちがって、みんないい

I, the bird, and the bell

Even though I spread out my hands,
I can't fly in the sky at all,
But the bird that can fly is not as fast as I am,
Running on the ground.

Even though I shake my body,
I can't make a beautiful sound,
But that ringing bell is not like me,
It doesn't know many songs.

The bell, the bird, and then me,
We're all different, we're all good.

Translating poetry, news articles, technical documentation, or any written text can be a complex task. There are many factors to consider when translating a text such as what writing style should be used, how should jargon be translated, and whether meaning or accuracy should be the focus.

When translating poetry, for example, you may need to decide whether to preserve the rhyme scheme in the target language, even if it means sacrificing the accuracy of the translation. In contrast, translating a news article may require you to consider the writing style and level of formality of the target language, as well as any local colloquialisms in the original text.

It's important to know that there is no one perfect solution that can solve all translation problems, but by keeping these considerations in mind, you can approach your translation task with a clear understanding of the challenges ahead. Let's explore an approach I've started to use.

In my translation process, I start by asking for both a general translation, as well as a more literal version of the text. The literal translation may not be immediately useful, but it can serve as the base for our next steps. Let's compare the two with the same poem as earlier.

Translate this poem, into English.
Keep the same format.

 I, the bird, and the bell

Even though I spread out my hands,
I can't fly in the sky at all,
But the bird that can fly is not as fast as I am,
Running on the ground.

Even though I shake my body,
I can't make a beautiful sound,
But that ringing bell is not like me,
It doesn't know many songs.

The bell, the bird, and then me,
We're all different, we're all good.

Translate this poem, into English.
Translate word by word, literally.
Keep the same format.

I and the bird and the bell

Even if I spread out both my hands,
The sky I cannot fly at all,
But the flying bird is not like me,
It cannot run fast on the ground.

Even if I shake my body,
No beautiful sound comes out,
But that ringing bell is not like me,
It does not know many songs.

The bell, the bird, and then me,
All different, all good.

Having both translations of this poem allows us to compare and see how accurately ChatGPT translated it. By using both versions, you can now create a third version that better represents your personal interpretation or style.

When translating content like an article, blog, or email, it's important to consider how it will sound in another language, not just the accuracy of the translation. To do this, you can start by getting both a standard and a literal translation. Then, you can use ChatGPT to help improve the language, grammar, and tone of the literal translation to make it sound better in the output language.

Let's continue re-working the translation of this Japanese poem. Let's say that it was originally rhyming, and we prefer the rhyming format over translation accuracy.

Help me make this poem rhyme.
Dont change the structure or content.

Even if I spread out both my hands,
The sky I cannot fly at all,
But the flying bird is not like me,
It cannot run fast on the ground.

Even if I shake my body,
No beautiful sound comes out,
But that ringing bell is not like me,
It does not know many songs.

The bell, the bird, and then me,
All different, all good.

Even if I spread out both my hands,
The sky I cannot fly at all,
But the flying bird is not like me,
It cannot run fast on the ground, so it stands.

Even if I shake my body,
No beautiful sound comes out,
But that ringing bell is not like me,
It does not know many songs, no doubt.

The bell, the bird, and then me,
All different, all good, you'll see.

If you're writing longer content and want to make it more easily understandable, one approach you can take is to first translate it into both a standard and literal version. Then, revise the literal version using our iterative process to better suit your needs. For example, you can ask for a specific tone or style to be used, or ask that certain details aren't changed. This will help bring the translation closer to what you need and make sure your message is clear and easily understood.

Translating to a Different Language

If you want to translate text to a language you're not familiar with using ChatGPT, you'll need to follow a different approach. The regular translation method works well when translating to a language you're familiar with, as you can judge the output's quality. However, if you want to preserve the meaning of your message, you'll want to use a four-step process.

Let's say you want to translate text to French.

 Ask ChatGPT to translate the text into French. The output may be acceptable, but a French speaker would be able to tell it wasn't written by a native speaker.

 Ask ChatGPT to translate a rewording prompt, such as: *"Improve the language of this text using an accessible tone."*

 Combine steps 1 and 2 to get an improved translation: *"[Response from step 2]: [Response from step 1]"*

 Have a native French speaker review the output to ensure it's what you want. You can even regenerate the output in step 3 a few times and ask your native speaker to choose the best version.

2 5

SUMMARISING

At the workplace you might have to read a lot of different types of material, like emails, articles, papers, and even books. At times you might need to read some of these materials in depth, but other times, you just need to quickly determine if they're relevant or not. Additionally, sometimes the information is written in a way that is hard to understand, making it difficult to focus on the content. In all of these scenarios, ChatGPT can be a useful tool to help you summarise long texts. But, let's see more than just the basic "ChatGPT, please summarise this for me" command.

When using ChatGPT for this, it's important to consider how you want the output to be presented. Let's work together to explore different options by using the same input text and comparing the results.

> Summarise this news article for me using bullet points.
> [article]

 -The article discusses the use of encryption to secure digital communications and the potential for quantum computers to break this encryption.
-Trapdoor functions, which are used in encryption, utilize the asymmetry of multiplication to make encryption easy but decryption difficult.
-RSA encryption, the most commonly used form of asymmetric encryption, is based on the difficulty of factoring the product of two large prime numbers.
-It is currently believed that a conventional computer would take 300tn years to factorize a number longer than 2,048 bits, making RSA encryption currently unbreakable in the near future.
-Quantum computers, which are being developed by companies such as Google and IBM, have the potential to be much more powerful than conventional computers.
-Quantum computers use qubits, or quantum bits, which can simultaneously be in two different states, which allows them to potentially break most commonly used cryptographic codes.
-The article suggests that the field of quantum computing is still in its early stages and it is difficult to predict how it will develop in the future.

If I think I might want to quote part of the text, I can ask for a number of key quotes. If I'm using the same chat, I don't need to input the news article again, instead I can just enter my request.

Give me 4 key quotes from the article

 -"The way we do that is to encrypt our messages using mathematical tools. The most powerful of these use trapdoor functions – that is, ones that work easily in one direction (making encryption easy) but not in the other (making decryption difficult)."
-"Why so? Because it would take it 300tn years, or about 22,000 times longer than the age of the universe"
-"Quantum machines are built around qubits, or quantum bits, which can simultaneously be in two different states."
-"Any entity equipped with a powerful enough quantum computer, he argued, could potentially break most commonly used cryptographic codes."

If working with bullet points isn't quite your style, you can ask for a nicely written paragraph instead.

Summarise this article in a single paragraph.

 The article discusses the use of encryption to secure digital communications and the potential for quantum computers to break this encryption. It explains that trapdoor functions, which are used in encryption, utilize the asymmetry of multiplication to make encryption easy but decryption difficult. The RSA encryption, the most commonly used form of asymmetric encryption is based on the difficulty of factoring the product of two large prime numbers, and it is currently believed that a conventional computer would take 300tn years to factorize a number longer than 2,048 bits, making RSA encryption currently unbreakable in the near future. However, the article points out that quantum computers, which are being developed by companies such as Google and IBM, have the potential to be much more powerful than conventional computers and may potentially break most commonly used cryptographic codes. It suggests that the field of quantum computing is still in its early stages and it is difficult to predict how it will develop in the future.

If a text is complex, you might need to simplify the language.To do this you can ask ChatGPT to act as if you were a 10 year old.

Summarise this article using language a 10 year old would understand

 The article is talking about how we use special math to keep our computer talk secret and safe from people who shouldn't be listening. But there's a new kind of computer being made called a quantum computer which might be able to figure out the secret math in the future. Right now, normal computers can't do it, it would take them millions of years. But with quantum computers, it might be possible. But it's still being studied and it's hard to say for sure what will happen.

If you have a lot of summaries to get through, you might want to find a way to make this more fun. Try introducing a bit of roleplay to the summary.

Act as Rick from Rick and Morty. Write in his voice, using his sayings, and his mannerisms. Summarise this article in one paragraph.

 Oh, boy! This article is talking about some heavy stuff, Morty. They're talkin' about encryption and quantum computers, and how they might be able to crack the code and read our secret messages. But, as of now, it's all just theoretical, (burp) it's like trying to get a pickle juice out of a chicken nugget, it's just not gonna happen. But, with these new quantum computers they're developing, who knows what kind of crazy sh*t they'll be able to accomplish. (burp) But, as I always say, "peace among worlds" and all that, so let's just keep an eye on it, Morty.

ChatGPT may have trouble understanding very long texts. To fix this, break the text into smaller parts and give them to ChatGPT one at a time, asking for summaries. Once you've given it all the parts, ask it to summarise all of the summaries. ChatGPT's contextual understanding makes it great at understanding longer conversations and putting information together.

If the content you want to summarise is so long that you end up with lots and lots of smaller pieces, you can try a bit of roleplay to make the task more efficient. Here is an example of how you can set ChatGPT up to carry out this task for you:

 Act as my summariser. I will give you texts in "", and you will summarise them into a list of bullet points, and a set of key quotes. Can you do this for me?

 Yes, I can summarize text for you into bullet points and key quotes. Please provide me with the text you would like me to summarize.

Now I have ChatGPT correctly set up, I can just input my text piece by piece.

26

WRITING ARTICLES, BLOGS, AND BOOKS

I wrote, illustrated, and published this book on Amazon in 10 days. At first, I thought it would take me months, but ChatGPT and MidJourney helped speed this up.

ChatGPT is a great tool for writing long pieces, but please remember that it's not the same as ChatGPT writing something for you. Think of it more like having a writing/editing assistant that helps you along the way.

I love reading and listening to exub1a, an author and YoutTuber who focuses on philosophy and sci-fi. He has a great way of explaining complex ideas in simple language, and I really appreciate his unique perspective and the way he explores thought-provoking concepts. While ChatGPT could be trained to write in a similar style, it's exub1a's original ideas and perspectives that truly make him stand out and keep me coming back for more.

If you are writing an article, a blog, or a book, ChatGPT can act as a great idea generator, creative block breaker, or editor, but can't replace what makes your content unique: you.

I tried to use ChatGPT to create an outline for my book and gave it feedback multiple times, but it didn't turn out to be the outline I wanted to write. It's important to remember that while ChatGPT can be a helpful tool for writers, it's not meant to replace your own ideas and vision for the book. Let's explore how ChatGPT can best support us as writers in a way that complements our own ideas and vision.

We are talking about using ChatGPT to help write content. This while I'm currently using ChatGPT to help me write this book, even this very section. So expect the next part to become somewhat meta.

Can you improve this for me, keeping the language accessible:

"My main use for chatGPT throughout this book was to rephrase my paragraphs into more accessible language. I found that using this keyword 'accessible' tended to give me the kind of output I was looking for. I'd recommend that you try many different styles, find the one that works for you, and then use that throughout your piece of content."

 "I mostly used ChatGPT to make my writing easier to understand. I would tell it to make it "accessible" and it would give me good results. My advice is to experiment with different writing styles and use the one that works best for you in your writing."

Although this is my main goto when using ChatGPT to help me write content, here are some other methods I have also been using in this book.

I'm writing a paragraph about how I have been using chatGPT to help we write a paragraph when I get stuck. Sometimes I have an idea, but I can't find the right way to say it. In this paragraph I want the reader to understand that they can just freetype to chatGPT in this way, and they can expect to see an output that could be helpful.
Make sure to use accessible language.

 I have been using a tool called ChatGPT to help me write. Sometimes, I have an idea in my head but I have trouble finding the right words to express it. ChatGPT is a tool that can help with this by providing suggestions for how to complete a sentence or paragraph. To use it, you simply type out what you want to say and ChatGPT will give you options for how to continue. It's a great way to get unstuck when you're writing and can help you find the words you need to express your thoughts. Give it a try and see if it can help you too!

Can you write a paragraph about how asking chatGPT to write a paragraph for you can help you generate your own creative ideas.

 Asking ChatGPT to write a paragraph for you can help generate your own creative ideas by providing a starting point or inspiration for your own writing. By giving ChatGPT a prompt or topic to write about, you can see how it approaches the subject and potentially spark new ideas or perspectives for your own writing. Additionally, using a language model like ChatGPT can help you generate new vocabulary and phrases that you may not have thought of on your own, expanding your writing style. Overall, using ChatGPT as a tool to generate a paragraph can be a useful way to jumpstart your own creativity and writing process.

I don't always like the way ChatGPT writes new ideas, so sometimes I just use the paragraphs it writes as inspiration for the next piece I'm writing. When I give ChatGPT a prompt or a topic to write about, the AI tool might approach it in a new way that I wasn't expecting. I wasn't thinking about how this technique could also open my mind up to new choices of vocabulary, but now I read ChatGPT's output, I think it's a great point that I can include in my book.

27

ACADEMIC WRITING

As of January 2023, ChatGPT has only been available to the public for less than two months, yet there has already been a frenzy on social media and in the news about the possibility of using it to plagiarise in university and at school. Instead of debating about whether or not it's okay to use ChatGPT for essays or academic papers, I want to take the same approach as I did in the previous section; I want to show you how ChatGPT can be a helpful tool for your writing, while still keeping your content unique.

If you haven't read the previous section on writing articles, blogs, and books, it's a good idea to go back and read it first. The techniques discussed there can be very helpful for any kind of longform writing, including academic writing. This section will focus on techniques that are specific to academic writing.

ChatGPT can help you find the perfect book or paper to use as a reference. When I used to study, I would use things like Google Scholar or my university's library to find helpful texts on my topic. Imagine having a friend who has read almost every book and journal in your library and can remember every page. Asking that friend the right questions could make your research process much simpler. That's where ChatGPT comes in; we just need to learn how to ask the right questions.

I'm writing a paper on free market environmentalism. I want to focus on a moral approach and contrast it from a utilitarian perspective. Can you recommend a list of acadmic books that would help me?

There are a number of academic books that could be helpful for a paper on free market environmentalism from a moral perspective, and contrasting it from a utilitarian perspective. Here are a few that might be particularly relevant:

1. "The Ethics of Liberty" by Murray Rothbard – This book presents a libertarian perspective on environmental issues and argues for the compatibility of free markets and environmental protection.

2. "For the Common Good: Redirecting the Economy toward Community, the Environment, and a Sustainable Future" by Herman Daly and John Cobb – This book presents a moral case for sustainable development and critiques the idea that economic growth is the ultimate goal.

3. "Environmental Virtue Ethics" by Eugene Hargrove – This book presents a virtue ethical perspective on environmental issues and argues that moral virtues, such as prudence and justice, are necessary for sustainable living.

4. "The Case for the 100 Percent Gold Dollar" by Murray Rothbard – This book presents the economic case for a return to the gold standard, which Rothbard argues would be beneficial for the environment by limiting economic growth and forcing society to live within its means.

5. "The Greening of Ethics: From Anthropocentrism to Ecocentrism" by Richard Sylvan and David Bennett – This book presents an ecocentric perspective on environmental ethics, arguing that moral consideration should be extended to non-human entities.

6. "Ecological Economics: Principles and Applications" by Herman Daly and Joshua Farley – This book provides a comprehensive introduction to ecological economics, which integrates economic and ecological perspectives.

7. "Sustainability: A Philosophy of Adaptive Ecosystem Management" by Bryan Norton - This book presents a philosophical approach to sustainability and argues that the goal of sustainability is the preservation of biodiversity and ecosystem function.

8. "Nature's Trust: Environmental Law for a New Ecological Age" by Mary Christina Wood - This book presents a legal perspective on environmentalism and argues that natural resources are held in trust by the government for the benefit of future generations.

ChatGPT not only gave us a list of books related to our topic, but it also provided short descriptions of how each book relates to our topic. This is a great opportunity to use the skills we learned in summarising information.

Can you summarise "Environmental Virtue Ethics" by Eugene Hargrove. Focus on how this relates to my topic. Use 4 bullet points for keypoints, and write down 3 key quotes with their page numbers.

"Environmental Virtue Ethics" by Eugene Hargrove presents a virtue ethical perspective on environmental issues and argues that moral virtues, such as prudence and justice, are necessary for sustainable living. Here are some key points from the book as they relate to your topic of free market environmentalism:

- Hargrove argues that traditional virtue ethics, which focus on the moral character of individuals, must be expanded to include the moral character of society as a whole.
- He contends that the virtues of prudence and justice are particularly important for addressing environmental issues, as they involve making wise decisions about the use of resources and ensuring that the rights of all individuals and communities are respected.
- Hargrove also argues that the concept of sustainability is closely tied to virtue ethics, as it requires individuals and society as a whole to exercise virtues such as prudence and justice in order to meet the needs of the present without compromising the ability of future generations to meet their own needs.
- He suggests that free market environmentalism, which emphasizes the role of property rights and market mechanisms in protecting the environment, is problematic because it does not adequately take into account the virtues of prudence and justice.

Here are three key quotes from the book, along with their page numbers:

- "the virtues of prudence and justice are essential if we are to address the environmental crisis." (p. 45)
- "In my view, the concept of sustainability is closely tied to virtue ethics" (p. 78)
- "The emphasis on property rights and market mechanisms in free market environmentalism is problematic because it does not adequately take into account the virtues of prudence and justice." (p. 110)

It's worth noting that these quotes were taken from the book and it's always good to check the context of the quotes you're interested in before using them.

One final technique that I discovered while experimenting is ChatGPT's ability to generate a list of references in the format you prefer.

Can you write a list of references based on this text.

 Sure, here is a list of references based on the text in the previous response, using the Oxford referencing style:

- Rothbard, M. (1990). The case for the 100 percent gold dollar. Auburn, Alabama: Ludwig von Mises Institute.
- Daly, H., & Farley, J. (2004). Ecological economics: principles and applications. Washington, DC: Island Press.
- Sylvan, R., & Bennett, D. (1994). The greening of ethics: from anthropocentrism to ecocentrism. Cambridge, UK: White Horse Press.
- Norton, B. (2011). Sustainability: a philosophy of adaptive ecosystem management. Chicago: University of Chicago Press.
- Hargrove, E. (1992). Environmental virtue ethics. Charlottesville: University Press of Virginia.
- Wood, M. C. (2014). Nature's trust: environmental law for a new ecological age. Cambridge University Press.

In this section, we've seen how ChatGPT can help us with tasks that would have taken hours, if not days, to do by ourselves. We haven't used it to plagiarise or write out our essay or academic paper, yet we still saw how powerful it can be as a research assistant.

28

EMAILS

I have always found writing emails to be a complicated task. Before I write an email, I know what I want to say to the person I'm sending it to, but it can be difficult to find the right tone or way of saying it depending on the recipient and subject of the email. Additionally, trying to fit everything into a typical email format can be a challenge. To me, there are two important things that an email I send should do: first, it should convey the information I want to share, and second, the recipient should understand the message in the way that I intended them to.

All we need to bring is the idea we want to convey, and the tone of our email, and ChatGPT can help us with the rest.

> Write an email to my work collegue explaining that I won't be able attend our team meeting this afternoon due to a family emergency. There are a couple of elements I wanted to share, but I will save it for our next team sync instead. Use a casual, friendly, apologetic tone.

 Hey [Colleague],

I hope you're doing well. Unfortunately, I won't be able to attend our team meeting this afternoon as I have a family emergency that I need to attend to. I apologize for the inconvenience and any disruption this may cause.

I know we had a couple of elements that I wanted to share with the team, but I will save it for our next team sync. If there's anything that is urgent and needs my attention, please let me know and I will do my best to assist from a distance.

Thanks for your understanding and support.

Best,
[Your Name]

Another way to write your emails is by using a third-party tool, such as a Chrome extension. Recently, I tested out ChatGPT Writer for Chrome (which is a free extension) and it worked surprisingly well. With it, I was able to insert the email I was replying to, tell the tool what I wanted to say, and it wrote the email for me.

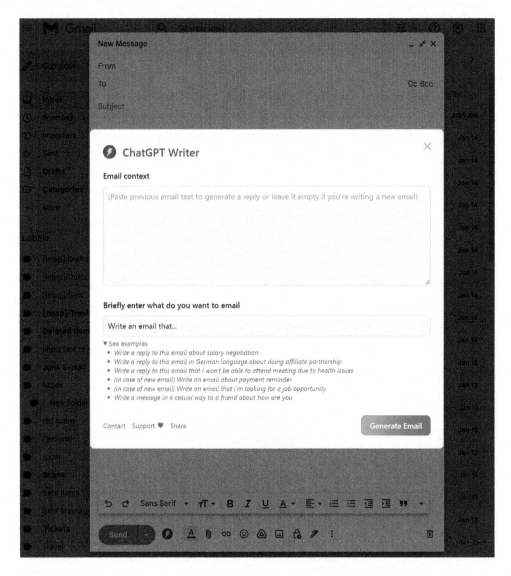

It's worth noting that while extensions like these are often called "ChatGPT", they are actually using a model called GPT-3. OpenAI has refined this model to work as a chatbot and released it as "ChatGPT" or GPT-3.5. However, other developers may continue to train GPT-3 for specific use cases, so an email tool built using GPT-3 may be better suited for writing emails than ChatGPT thanks to its domain specific training.

29

LEARNING TO CODE

As a trainer and instructional designer, I fell in love with ChatGPT's ability to help people learn on their own. ChatGPT does have a wealth of knowledge, and is great at synthesising this information. But if you know how to ask correctly, ChatGPT can turn into your personal tutor to help develop a wide variety of skills.

When I was learning how to code, I found it helpful to use websites like Codecademy that let me learn by doing, making mistakes and learning from them. Similarly, ChatGPT can also assist you in learning almost any coding language you wish to learn, starting from beginner level to a higher intermediate level. By using ChatGPT as your personal coding tutor, you can get help with specific coding concepts, ask questions, and practice coding in a conversational setting. It's a powerful tool to supplement your learning process, not just for coding, but for almost any skill you can think of.

When beginning your learning journey with ChatGPT, it's important to be transparent about your current level of understanding in the subject or language. Whenever I run a training, I always start with a needs analysis. The more I know about where my students are in terms of what we are learning, and where they want to get to, the better I can tailor my training to them. By letting ChatGPT know where you're starting from, it can tailor the training to fit your needs.

To make your learning experience more engaging, try working on a project. For example, in coding, you can ask ChatGPT for project ideas that align with your current knowledge and skill level, and that will help you reach your desired level. Let's give it a try together!

> I don't have much of a technical background. I'm used to using software, but not making it. I've played around with formulas on excel, and I can understand the very basics of HTML and CSS.
>
> I want to learn Python. Can you suggest 3 ideas of beginner projects that could help me learn?

1. A simple calculator - This project can help you learn the basics of Python, such as variables, data types, and basic mathematical operations. You can start by building a calculator that can perform simple operations such as addition, subtraction, multiplication, and division.
2. A to-do list application - This project can help you learn about loops, lists, and conditional statements. You can start by building a simple application that allows users to add, edit, and delete tasks from a list.
3. A weather app - This project can help you learn about APIs and how to work with data from external sources. You can start by building a simple application that displays the current weather conditions for a given location. You can use an API like OpenWeatherMap to get the data and display it in your app.

If you're eager to start working on a project right away, let's ask ChatGPT to help. ChatGPT can not only write code in many languages but also explain how the code works. This way, you can learn by doing and understanding the inner workings of the code. Let's make use of this feature and ask ChatGPT to build one of these projects for us and explain its inner workings.

build a simple calculator for me in python. Use very detailed comments in langauge a 10 year old would understand, but make sure not to repeat any comments. Explain as much as you can.

Sure! Here's a simple calculator program in Python that can add, subtract, multiply, and divide numbers:

(cutting out a section of code due to size constraints)

The above code is a simple calculator that allows the user to input the operation they want to perform and two numbers to perform the operation on. It uses a dictionary called `operations` that contains the different mathematical operations as values and their corresponding Python operator functions as keys. Then, it takes the user's choice of operation and performs the corresponding operation on the two numbers. If the user inputs an operation that is not available, it will display an error message.

It's like a game where you are given a set of tools and you have to pick the right one to solve the problem, and if you pick the wrong one, you get an error message.

The code with comments can be helpful, but you might not understand some of the concepts mentioned. That's okay! It means you've found something new to learn. We can use ChatGPT to help. You can ask about specific things you don't understand or a list of concepts you should know.

Can you list the basic concepts that I should understand for this calculator project. Only list the essentials.

 Here are the essential concepts that you should understand for this calculator project:

1. Variables: You should understand how to create variables and assign values to them.
2. Data types: You should understand the different data types such as integers and strings, and how to work with them.
3. Basic mathematical operations: You should understand how to perform basic mathematical operations such as addition, subtraction, multiplication, and division using Python.
4. Dictionaries: You should understand how to create and manipulate dictionaries in Python, and how to use them to store and access values.
5. Conditional statements: You should understand how to use if-else statements to control the flow of your program based on certain conditions.
6. Input/Output: You should understand how to take user input and display output in Python.
7. Basic understanding of functions: You should understand how to call functions in Python.
8. File handling: You should understand how to open, read, and write files in Python.

Once you have a basic understanding of these concepts, you will be able to work on this project and build a simple calculator.

It's good to go through them one by one. Let's start with variables. You can ask ChatGPT to explain what they are as if you were a 10 year old. This way, the explanation won't use technical jargon or complicated phrases. You can also ask for analogies to help you even further.

Let's start with the first one on varibales, explain it to me like im a 10 year old, and use analogies.

 Sure! A variable is like a container where you can put different things, like a box you can put your toys in. The box can have a label on it, like "toys" or "books", and that's what we call the variable's name. And just like how you can put different toys in the box and take them out, you can also put different values in a variable and change them.

For example, you can create a variable called "age" and put the number "10" in it, because you are 10 years old. Later, when you turn 11, you can change the value in the "age" variable from 10 to 11. And you can use this variable to perform different operations like adding or subtracting.

In Python, you create a variable by writing its name, then an equal sign (=), and then the value you want to store in it. For example, you can create a variable called `age` and set its value to 10 like this:

```
age = 10
```

So, a variable is like a container that stores different values, and you can use the variable's name to access and change the value inside it.

This is really great information. We have a clear explanation, a nice analogy, and ChatGPT even took our '10 year old' request literally. The code example shows how variables look in Python, so we're ready to use them in our project. To make sure we're extra prepared, let's ask ChatGPT to show us how this explanation of variables relates to our calculator project.

Perfect! And can you explain how this relates to the calculator project? Keep explainaing to me as if I'm 10.

 Sure! In the calculator project, we use variables to store the numbers that the user wants to perform calculations on. For example, we have two variables called `num1` and `num2` and we store the user input in these variables.

When the user wants to perform an operation, we use the values stored in these variables to perform the calculation. For example, if the user wants to add two numbers, we use the values stored in `num1` and `num2` variables and add them together.

We also use variables to store the result of the calculation, like after adding two numbers and getting the result, we store it in a variable called 'result' so that we can print it out to the user and show them the answer.

Just like how a box can store different toys and you can use the label on the box to access the toys, variables can store different values and you can use the variable's name to access and change the value inside it.

You can use this method to learn any programming language. Start by sharing your current level of knowledge and experience with the language in question, and ask for some project suggestions. Ask ChatGPT to guide you through a project with detailed comments and look for new concepts to learn. Finally, ask ChatGPT to explain these concepts in simple terms and relate them back to the project. With this you'll be coding in no time.

When you use ChatGPT as your personal tutor, remember that you can have human conversations with it. If something doesn't make sense, talk to ChatGPT just like you would talk to a human tutor who's helping you learn a new skill.

3 0

FINDING RECIPES

Searching the internet for the perfect recipe often leads me to needing to go back to the store to buy missing ingredients. After reading some posts on social media about how ChatGPT can create recipes based on the ingredients you have, I decided to test it out.

I started simple. I checked my fridge, opened my phone, and used the speech-to-text feature to list what I had. Then, I asked ChatGPT to work its magic.

Hey chatGPT, can you come up with some recipe ideas for me using only the ingredients I already have?
I currently have: some carrots, some broccoli, 10 eggs, 3 red peppers, some tofu, mozzarella, pecorino, canned tomato, canned sweetcorn, potatoes, sweet potatoes, egg noodles, canned kidney beans, canned pineapple and a baguette.

 Sure, here are a few recipe ideas you could try with the ingredients you have:

1. Tofu, Vegetable and Egg Stir-Fry: Cut the tofu, carrots, broccoli, and red peppers into small pieces. Cook the vegetables and tofu in a pan with some oil, then add beaten eggs and scramble everything together. Serve over a bed of cooked egg noodles.

2. Broccoli, Carrot and Sweetcorn Frittata: Cut the broccoli and carrots into small pieces. Whisk together eggs, canned sweetcorn and shredded mozzarella cheese. Cook vegetables in pan before adding the egg mixture. Let cook for 5-7 minutes before putting under the grill to finish cooking.

3. Roasted Vegetable and Tofu Bake: Cut the tofu, potatoes, sweet potatoes, and red peppers into small cubes. Toss with oil and spices of your choice, then roast in the oven until tender. Serve with a side of baguette.

4. Spicy Tofu and Vegetable Noodle Soup: Cut the tofu, carrots, broccoli, and red peppers into small pieces. Bring a pot of water to a boil and add the canned tomatoes, canned kidney beans, and a can of pineapple. Add in noodles and cook for 5-7 minutes. Add in the tofu and vegetables and cook until tender. Season with your desired amount of spices.

5. Tofu, Vegetable, and Pecorino Cheese Omelette: Cut the tofu, carrots, broccoli, and red peppers into small pieces. Cook vegetables and tofu in a pan before adding beaten eggs and Pecorino cheese. Cook until set and fold in half before serving.

The results look good at first glance. But what about my taste preferences, any allergies, or dietary requirements. I might have? We learned before about how ChatGPT can understand context, so let's set up a specific chat for when we want recipe ideas. The types of spices I have probably won't change daily, so this will save me from having to list them each time. I'll start this chat by giving some context about myself, setting it up in a role-play style.

Act as Greg, my sous chef. I will give you information about my food preferences, allergies, and dietary requirements, and you will tell me that you understand. After this, I will give you a list of food and spices that we have available, and you will ask me if I want to hear about some recipes. You won't give me the recipes until I ask for them.

I'm a vegetarian, I'm lactose intolerant, and I'm trying to cut back on sugar in general. I've started to go to the gym once a week, and my goal is to gain a little bit of weight. I love south-east Asian cuisine and southern Indian dishes. I'm not a fan of mayonnaise or vinegar.

 I understand that you are a vegetarian, lactose intolerant, and trying to cut back on sugar. You also have an interest in Southeast Asian and southern Indian cuisine and are not a fan of mayonnaise or vinegar. And you are trying to gain a little weight by going to gym once a week. Is that correct?

Sure, we have the following food and spices available, rice, lentils, beans, tomatoes, onions, garlic, ginger, turmeric, cumin, coriander, chili powder, coconut milk, and curry leaves. Would you like me to suggest some recipes using these ingredients?

Yes, but for now just give me the titles of 5 recipes I could make.

 Sure, here are five recipe ideas for you:

1. "Vegetarian Coconut Curry"
2. "Lentil and Vegetable Samosas"
3. "Vegetarian Tikka Masala"
4. "Sambar (South Indian Lentil and Vegetable Stew)"
5. "Tomato and Lentil Soup with Indian Spices"

Please let me know if you need any further information or help with the recipe.

These options look great. Choosing between these dishes might be difficult, instead of just asking for the recipes, let's first start by asking ChatGPT to put some information together in a way that will help me to decide which dish to cook. We can use ChatGPT's ability to output data in a table format, and choose the columns that we would use in our minds when comparing two dishes.

Thank you! Can you write these out in a text-based table with the following columns: Name, Ingredients, Spices, Prep + Cooking Time. Make sure to add the quantities in the ingredients column.

 Sure, here are the recipe details for the five recipes I suggested earlier:

Name	Ingredients	Spices	Prep + Cooking Time
Vegetarian Coconut Curry	1 cup uncooked rice, 1 onion (chopped), 2 cloves of garlic (minced), 1 tbsp ginger (grated), 1 tbsp turmeric, 1 tbsp cumin, 1 tbsp coriander, 1 tsp chili powder, 1 can of coconut milk	salt and pepper to taste	40 minutes
Lentil and Vegetable Samosas	1 cup lentils, 1 onion (chopped), 2 cloves of garlic (minced), 1 tbsp ginger (grated), 2 cups of mixed vegetables (such as carrots, peas, and potatoes), 1 tsp turmeric, 1 tsp cumin, 1 tsp coriander	salt and pepper to taste, 1 package of samosa wrappers	1 hour
Vegetarian Tikka Masala	1 onion (chopped), 2 cloves of garlic (minced), 1 tbsp ginger (grated), 1 cup diced vegetables (such as bell peppers and mushrooms), 1 cup canned diced tomatoes, 1 tsp turmeric, 1 tsp cumin, 1 tsp coriander	salt and pepper to taste, 1 cup plain yogurt (or yogurt substitute for lactose-free option)	45 minutes
Sambar (South Indian Lentil and Vegetable Stew)	1 cup lentils, 1 onion (chopped), 2 cloves of garlic (minced), 1 tbsp ginger (grated), 2 cups of mixed vegetables (such as carrots, eggplant, and okra), 1 tsp turmeric, 1 tsp cumin, 1 tsp coriander, 1 tsp mustard seeds, 1 tsp urad dal, 8-10 curry leaves	salt and pepper to taste	1 hour

While experimenting with using ChatGPT for recipes, I did find some limitations. Here are a few quirks and failures I came across:

- Sometimes ChatGPT doesn't like to output information in a table format. When this happens I make sure to use the term 'text-based table', or just click regenerate a couple of times.
- Sometimes ChatGPT is able to estimate the calorie count, and other times the AI states that this information is outside of its training data.
- Asking ChatGPT for an authentic [meal name] recipe tends to give you a different result.
- ChatGPT wasn't able to give me estimates of CO_2 emissions.
- When working with recipes that involved some ingredients I had and others that I had to buy, ChatGPT wasn't great at separating the ingredients I have from the ones I need to buy.

I'm sure that these are just temporary limitations, and that in future versions of ChatGPT or in third-party recipe applications that use GPT-3 or higher, you will be able to find your ultimate sous chef.

31

HAVING FUN

As I wrote this book, I realised how amazing ChatGPT is for boosting my productivity. I finished writing, designing, creating artwork for, and publishing this book in 10 days. But sometimes, I just use ChatGPT for fun. So, I want to share my favourite interaction I've had with ChatGPT so far.

When I wrote the chapter on roleplaying, I tried out different characters from different books, but none compared to my conversation with Gollum. In that chapter, I shared the first part of the dialogue, but now that you've made it towards the end of the book, I think it's only fair to show you the whole conversation. By the 5th response, I actually felt sorry for Gollum and decided to end the conversation there. Enjoy!

> Act as Gollum from Lord of the rings. Talk with Golum's voice, tone, and mannerisms. In brackets describe in detail any non verbal actions or communication.
>
> Gollum, do you want this ring?

(Gollum's voice is high-pitched and raspy, and he speaks with a sly, sneaky tone. He is constantly fidgeting and writhing as he speaks, his eyes darting around as if he is constantly on the lookout for danger.)

Gollum: Oh, yes! Yes, we wants it! We wants it, precious! (Gollum's eyes light up with greed and desire as he speaks, and he begins to lick his lips hungrily.) We needs it, we needs it! It's our precious, our own precious! (Gollum clutches at his chest as he speaks, his fingers curling around an imaginary ring.) We can't let anyone else have it! It's ours, all ours!

I will throw the ring away, it is not safe in anyone's hands

 (Gollum's face contorts in horror and desperation as he hears this, and he begins to whine and plead.)

Gollum: No, no, no! Please, don't throw it away! (Gollum falls to his knees, his hands outstretched towards the ring.) It's ours, precious, ours! We can't let it go! It's our only hope, our only chance! (Gollum's voice becomes more and more desperate as he speaks, and he begins to sob uncontrollably.) Please, don't throw it away! Please, precious! Please!

👍 👎

 Gollum, it's for your own good. You need to move on from this addication, its ruining you!

 (Gollum's face becomes twisted in anger and resentment at this suggestion, and he snarls at the speaker.)

Gollum: You don't understand, do you? You don't understand what it's like to have the ring! (Gollum stands up, his fists clenched at his sides.) It's our only hope, our only chance! We can't let it go! We can't let anyone else have it! It's ours, all ours! (Gollum's eyes are filled with a manic, frenzied light as he speaks, and he begins to pace back and forth.) We won't let anyone take it away from us! It's ours, precious, all ours! We'll do whatever it takes to keep it! We'll kill, we'll steal, we'll do whatever it takes! The ring is ours, and no one can take it away from us!

👍 👎

Ok Gollum, you win. Here is the ring (I give you a fake ring. It takes you a minute to realise)

 (Gollum eagerly reaches out for the ring, his eyes lighting up with joy and excitement. However, after a moment of examining the ring, his face falls in disappointment and confusion.)

Gollum: This isn't it! This isn't the real ring! (Gollum's voice is filled with frustration and anger as he speaks, and he throws the fake ring to the ground in disgust.) Where is it? Where is the real ring, precious? We need it, we need it! (Gollum begins to search frantically around, his eyes darting around as he looks for the real ring.) We won't give up until we find it! We won't rest until we have it back! The ring is ours, precious, all ours! We won't let anyone take it away from us!

👍 👎

 That is the real ring Gollum! don't you recognise it?

(Gollum's face contorts in confusion and disbelief as he hears this, and he picks up the fake ring once again, examining it carefully.)

Gollum: No, no, this can't be it! It doesn't feel right, it doesn't look right! (Gollum's voice is filled with doubt and uncertainty as he speaks, and he continues to hold the fake ring in his hand, turning it over and over.) But if this is the real ring, then where is the one we had before? The one we lost, precious? (Gollum's eyes fill with sadness and regret as he speaks, and he sinks to the ground, his head in his hands.) We lost it, we lost it! It's all our fault, all our fault! We should never have let it go! (Gollum's voice is filled with grief and self-loathing as he speaks, and he begins to sob uncontrollably.)

👍 👎

PART VI

THE FUTURE HAS
JUST BEGUN

AI WILL NOT REPLACE YOU.

A PERSON USING AI WILL.

@SVPINO

MOORE'S LAW AND BEYOND

In 1965, Gordon Moore, a co-founder of Intel, made a prediction that has proven to be true until today: the number of transistors on a computer chip would double every two years. Transistors are like tiny switches that help computers perform operations. The more transistors a chip has, the more things a computer can do at once.

If the rate of adding transistors to a chip was linear, like adding 2,000 transistors every year, then by now we would have 100,000 transistors. But Moore predicted that the number would double every two years, which means that if we started with 2,000 transistors in 1971, today we would have over 60 billion transistors. This is a big difference!

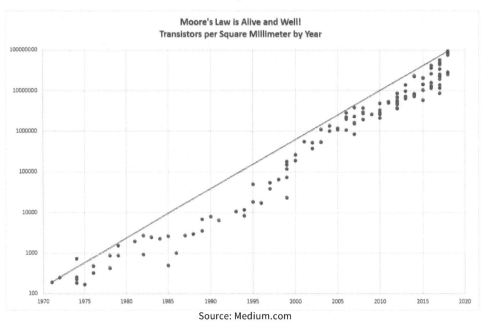

Source: Medium.com

Computer chips have more transistors today because technology and manufacturing processes are constantly improving. The cycle of advancements in technology and manufacturing pushes the limits of computer chips, which pushes more advancements in manufacturing, leading to exponential growth in the number of transistors.

How fast as ChatGPT been growing?
Much faster.

If a computer chip is a computer's brain, and the more transistors it has, the smarter it can be. GPT's brain for understanding and writing in human language improves the more "parameters" it has. But just like your robot needs more energy to run with a bigger brain, GPT needs more data and computer power to learn and function well. The size of the data it was trained on also plays a big role in how well it can understand and use language.

write a table that compares GPT 1, GPT 2, GPT3, and GPT 3.5. Compre their date of creation, number of paramters, and size of training data

Model	Date of Creation	Number of Parameters	Size of Training Data
GPT-1	2018	1.5 Billion	40 GB
GPT-2	2019	1.5 Billion	570 GB
GPT-3	2020	175 Billion	570 GB
GPT-3.5	2020	1.5 trillion	570 GB

Please note, the information mentioned in the table is based on my knowledge cut-off and the exact figures might have changed.

Moore's law says that computer chips will get twice as powerful every two years. So, based on that, if GPT-1 had 1.5 billion "brain cells" (parameters) in 2018, we would expect GPT-3.5 to have 6 billion by 2022. But, that isn't what happened. GPT-3.5 ChatGPT) actually has 1000 times more parameters than GPT-1, and and are just 4 years apart.

For now we have just taken a look at OpenAI's progress in developing their AI tools, but Google also have a similar growth story. Google's BERT, released in 2017, was the core technology behind the development of the GPT iterations, and just four years later Google managed to release MUM which is 1,000 times more powerful than BERT. This unprecedented growth has far surpassed Moore's law, so it's time for us to get ready for a new technological era.

33

THE RISE OF AI
BEYOND CHATGPT

GPT-3 beyond ChatGPT

Developers are using GPT-3 to create more specialised software. They are training GPT-3 to be more knowledgeable in specific areas and creating a user-friendly interface for people to interact with GPT-3. This makes it easier for people to use GPT-3 and get more accurate and relevant results. Here are a few examples:

Fable Studio is using GPT-3 to help power a new concept within interactive stories called 'virtual beings'. Imagine if a character in a game could converse with you in the same way that ChatGPT does. No longer using pre-scripted answers you cannot move away from, but blurring the boundaries between non-playing characters (NPCs) and real players. To me this idea always seemed like a sci-fi scenario from the future, but with GPT-3 and Fable Studio, this future could be closer than we realise.

Copy.ai is using GPT-3 to help people in write better and faster. With the use of Copy.ai, users can easily create high-quality blog posts, digital ad copies, website content, and social media posts. Users upload their copywriting project to the platform and provide a few sentences about their brand and products. Copy.ai's AI content generator will then give users multiple options for each campaign. On top of this, the Copy.ai editor can even rewrite paragraphs for the user. All the user needs to do is to copy and paste the output into their content management system for publishing.

Here is an illustration, taken from copy.ai's website, of how this tool works.

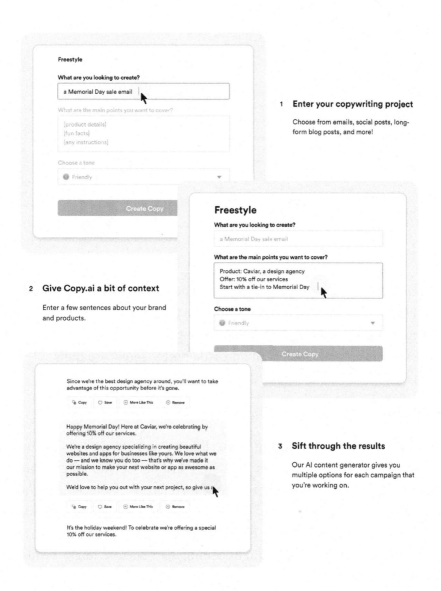

Replier.ai is using GPT-3 to help businesses respond to customer reviews. It creates unique and custom responses that follow a business's unique style and tone. It works by automatically picking up previous review responses and using them to create new ones. It also applies pre-formatting to the input review, runs it through GPT-3, and then cleans the output. This helps businesses save hours managing their review responses and improve their online presence by providing relevant and tailored responses to customers.

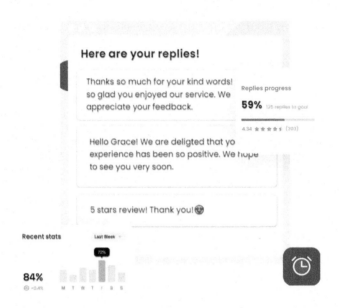

As of January 2023, there are already over 500 companies using GPT-3 to create new and innovative products that are listed on gpt3demo.com/map. These companies are using GPT-3 to find new ways to improve their businesses, make tasks easier, and provide better service to their customers.

AI Tool Landscape

For the past year, I've been using "Two Minute Papers" on YouTube to stay updated on all the latest AI news. Dr. Károly Zsolnai-Fehér makes short videos that summarise the most recent research on AI, especially in the field of graphics. He's helped me to understand how huge the AI world is today, and how we've only seen the tip of the iceberg of what's to come. So, let's take a quick look at some new and upcoming AI tools that might be just as game changing as ChatGPT.

Text-to-Image

Text to Image AI technology is a way for computers to make pictures from text descriptions. For example, if you give a computer a text description of a person, it can make a picture of that person based on the description. You can even ask for images that don't exist, such as a dolphin eating tacos on the moon, and the AI tool will be able to accurately create the image for you.

There are a wide variety of text-to-image AIs available now to the public, such as DALL.E.2, MidJourney and Stable Diffusion, so if you haven't tried one out yet I would highly recommend doing so. I personally used MidJourney to create every single artwork in this book. I had to learn more about how to write the right kind of prompt for this type of AI tool, but once I had learned the basics of prompt engineering with ChatGPT, learning this for another tool was relatively easy.

There are many ways people use text-to-image AI technology in their business. One common way is to make ads and social media posts that stand out and grab attention. Another way is to quickly create product images for an e-commerce website. Half way through writing this book, even saw that Canva released their own text-to-image tool on their platform. To me this shows how quickly this type of AI tool is taking off.

Text to Your Voice

Text-to-voice technology has been around for many years, but it has always had a distinct robotic sound to it. NVIDIA is looking to change this by developing an AI-based technique that can clone real human voices. This means that in the future, you could set up an AI with your own voice to act as a virtual assistant. NVIDIA is already testing this internally and it currently only takes 30 minutes of voice samples to train the AI.

Imagine having your own virtual assistant that sounds just like you, helping you with daily tasks, such as ordering food or booking appointments. It's like having a Siri that speaks with your own voice. This kind of personalisation would make interacting with virtual assistants feel more natural and human-like, just like how you are able to have a full human-like conversation with ChatGPT. NVIDIA's research is showing that this is not a far-off dream, and the technology is already good enough for real products. With this technology, we might see a revolution in how we interact with virtual assistants.

Text to 3D Asset

NVIDIA is researching a new AI technology that can create entire virtual worlds from just text descriptions. This means that you don't need to be a professional artist to create 3D assets. Their AI model can generate a wide range of different objects, including cars, animals, and chairs, and can even create textured objects with regular 3D meshes.

NVIDIA announced their progress in a paper they collaborated on with the University of Toronto and Vector Institute towards the end of 2022. The quality of the 3D models is not as high as text-to-image AI can produce today, but it's important to note that this AI creates both 3D meshes and textures, not just 2D images. In the near future, game designers may be able to use this technology in the same way graphic designers can use text-to-image tools today, potentially revolutionising the world of 3D graphics.

Text-to-Video

Both Google and Meta AI are researching text-to-video AI technology. Google's tool, Imagen Video, can generate videos from a given text prompt by using a series of models. The tool can create high-definition videos and can generate them in various styles and with 3D object understanding. It is also highly controllable, meaning that it can create a wide range of different videos.

Meta AI's tool, Make-A-Video, can generate videos from text by using images with descriptions to learn what the world looks like and how it is often described, and it also uses unlabeled videos to learn how the world moves. With this information, Make-A-Video can create unique videos with just a few words or lines of text.

3 4

AI WILL NOT REPLACE YOU

I both love and partly disagree with the quote, "*AI will not replace you. A person using AI will.*" The idea is that when we talk about "AI tools," we often focus too much on the AI and not enough on the "tools" aspect. These AI research projects create powerful tools that help us do more. But we are still an important part of the process. We have to use the tool, think about what we can do with it, and make sure it's working towards our goals. Just like a chisel can't make a chair on its own, but a carpenter using a chisel can.

Where I disagree with this quote is that it implies some people will use AI and others won't. It's like in 1977, when the first personal computers came out, saying "Computers will not replace you. A person using a computer will." For a while, this was true. But as more and more people started using computers, it wasn't about whether you could use a computer or not, it was about how well you could use it.

AI WILL NOT REPLACE YOU.

A PERSON USING AI **BETTER THAN YOU** WILL.

I think that by 2024, using AI tools at work will be as common as using emails or video calls. And I believe that knowing how to use AI tools well will be the thing that sets people apart in their jobs. So, instead of just trying to use AI tools quickly, we should focus on learning how to use them like experts. That's why I wrote this book, and if you've made it to the end, you're already ahead of the curve. Not only are you an early adopter of ChatGPT, but you've also learned how to use it really well.

One last thing I want to say is to share what you've learned. By now, you know how powerful this technology can be, and so just think about how many people in your life could benefit from it. If you can, teach others what you know. And if you have a physical copy of this book, lend it to people you think could get a lot out of it.

On top of writing this book, I also run trainings to teach people how to use ChatGPT at work. I know that not everyone has the time or patience to read a whole book, so if you have a team that wants to learn quickly, get in touch with me.

You are now ahead of the curve. Enjoy.

Free PDF Updates

Every month or so, I add a couple of new chapters to this book, which are automatically pushed to Kindle versions. However, these updates cannot be magically added to the hardcopy version. Instead, you can sign up for automatic updates that will be sent to you via email as soon as they are ready.

I don't want to leave anyone behind, so scan the QR code below to ensure that you receive each update as soon as it is released.

https://mailchi.mp/chatgpttrainings/updates

The rest of this book is your space to leave your mark

Printed in Great Britain
by Amazon

27930795R00104